Hutcheson Macaulay Posnett

The Historical Method in Ethics, Jurisprudence, and Political Economy

Hutcheson Macaulay Posnett

The Historical Method in Ethics, Jurisprudence, and Political Economy

ISBN/EAN: 9783337319700

Printed in Europe, USA, Canada, Australia, Japan

Cover: Foto ©ninafisch / pixelio.de

More available books at **www.hansebooks.com**

THE HISTORICAL METHOD

IN

ETHICS, JURISPRUDENCE, AND POLITICAL ECONOMY,

BY

HUTCHESON MACAULAY POSNETT, M. A.,

LATE SENIOR CLASSICAL MODERATOR,
UNIVERSITY SCHOLAR, WALL ORIENTAL SCHOLAR,
DUBLIN UNIVERSITY.

'As what he sees is, so have his thoughts been.'

LONDON:
LONGMANS, GREEN, AND CO.
1882.

[*Rights of Translation and Reproduction reserved.*]

TO

THE MASTER OF TRINITY HALL,

CAMBRIDGE.

PREFACE.

THERE is a question underlying all Historical Philosophy, What is the relation of the Individual to Society, to the Species; are their Interests, are their Consciences, Identical? The Historical Method has presented that question in its naked form. But the nature and limits of the Method have been left undefined, and the absence of links between Historical Philosophy and the Philosophy of Mind has unfavourably affected the progress of both. In attempting to construct a Social History of a certain Semitic nation, the vagueness of the Method as now understood constantly forced itself upon my attention, and the following pages represent an effort to correct that vagueness, to prove that the Historical Method is in harmony with Inductive Science, that its essential characteristic is the Reversal of Mental Evolution, and that the Philosophy of the Finite and the Historical Philosophy are One.

  24, TRINTIY COLLEGE, DUBLIN,
    March 15*th*, 1882.

CONTENTS.

CHAPTER I.

THE NATURE AND LIMITS OF THE HISTORICAL METHOD.

	Page.
EXPERIENCE AND THEORY, ...	1–4
SUBORDINATE SPECIES OF THE HISTORICAL METHOD,	5–10
THE REASON OF THE HISTORICAL METHOD,	11–22

CHAPTER II.

THE HISTORICAL METHOD IN ETHICS.

THE PRACTICAL VALUE OF HISTORICAL ETHICS.	23–30
THE ETHICS OF MR. MILL, . .	30–34
THE ETHICS OF MR. HERBERT SPENCER,	34–48
PROBABLE FUTURE OF HISTORICAL ETHICS,	49–51

CHAPTER III.

THE HISTORICAL METHOD IN JURISPRUDENCE.

THE HISTORICAL METHOD AND MR. BENTHAM,	52–56
THE HISTORICAL METHOD AND MR. AUSTIN,	56–58
THE HISTORICAL METHOD AND SIR HENRY MAINE, .	58–75

CHAPTER IV.

THE HISTORICAL METHOD IN POLITICAL ECONOMY.

	Page.
THE METHODS OF ECONOMIC SCIENCE,	76–79
ECONOMIC ORTHODOXY AND THE HISTORICAL METHOD,	79–108

CHAPTER V.

THE LOGIC OF THE HISTORICAL METHOD.

THE HISTORICAL METHOD AND DEDUCTION,	109–111
THE HISTORICAL METHOD AND INDUCTION,	111, 112
THE DEVELOPMENT OF THE THREE METHODS,	112–115

NOTE, ... 117, 118

THE HISTORICAL METHOD

IN

ETHICS, JURISPRUDENCE, AND POLITICAL ECONOMY.

CHAPTER I.

THE NATURE AND LIMITS OF THE HISTORICAL METHOD.

THERE is a god before whom sackbut, psaltery, and all manners of music are played and have long been played, before whom the tamest and wildest genuflexions have been performed, and shall no doubt be long performed. His name is Theory. His servants are legion. Politics, Religion, Philosophy, all bow to his laws. What is this magnificent deity so widely worshipped? An abstraction, a generalization, a creed, a constitution.

There is another god who, from the insignificance of an autochthon, has grown into the rival of that universal deity, and extended his pretensions from insignificance beyond the very bounds of Human Associations. His name is Experience. His servants have swelled from a few respectful retainers into an adoring multitude that no man can number. Yet there was a time when his very existence was unknown, or at least disregarded. In an ancient world, replete with miracles of mind and matter, man, the slave of an uncontrolled imagination, and the sport of inexplicable mysteries, yielded to Theory a sovereignty as vague and unlimited as his own conception of life. But step by step the earth-born upstart has circumscribed the vagueness of that universal sovereignty, expanded the range of his own influences, and at last threatened to usurp the eternal titles of his superb rival. What is this earth-born upstart? A fact, a number, a quantity, a sensation.

The servants of these rival gods, determined never to part the sovereignty, have declared a peaceless war, the oldest war in the world, and bent upon mutual annihilation, have scarcely contemplated the possibility of a compromise. But amidst the conflict of limitless pretensions, a party of compromise has at length appeared, and this is their message :— There are not two gods but one god, and his godship is limited. Now this was the way the Unitarian secret had leaked out. Servants of Theory had enjoyed an occasional glance of disdain at Experience, as they encountered his satellites; and at last some of them ventured to report that he looked very like Theory *done in large*. On the other hand, servants of Experience came back with a cock-and-bull story of their enemy's exceeding likeness to Experience, *done in small*. And at last both reports were so noised abroad, that some ventured to proclaim their Unitarian faith, and the party of reconciliation and compromise arose.

But there was a sect of Theory-worshippers, a militant

sect, who could never agree to this reconciliation, whose absolute dogma was that Theory is divine, that Experience is mortal. Of such divinity, each one of this militant sect recognised himself as more or less a fragment, or rather himself as the more, and others as the less. And, strange to say, the most abject servants of Experience said they worshipped him only in so far as he was mortal, and loudly asserted that in everything else they were the devotees of Theory alone. Thus extremes met, and the battle of the gods assumed a more portentous form than ever. There was defection everywhere. There was hypocrisy everywhere. And worse than all, there are millions in both camps who cannot clearly see why they are in either. Meanwhile, the Unitarian heretics are hard at work. Little by little they are comparing Theory with Experience, and reducing both to the limits of the Finite. And lately they have openly said that from the crown of his head to the sole of his foot, from the newest patch to the oldest rag he wears, Theory has worn, and is wearing the clothes of Experience *cut down*, the clothes which Experience in many places and ages wears or has thrown aside.

Such is the battle of the Absolute Philosophies, the dogmatic Philosophy of Matter, the dogmatic Philosophy of Mind, and such is the compromise of the Relative Philosophy. Let us secede from that field of confusion. Let us fraternise with those who make for peace. We have seceded, then, we have joined their ranks. But we are still in search of truth. What truth? Not Absolute Truth linked by a causation to Physical Force: not Absolute Truth linked by causation to

Eternal Mind. What then is *our* truth, or rather, what are *our truths*? For about the abstract entity we fight no longer. The truths of Social and Individual relations—Relative Truths. We refuse to connect them with the divine or the eternal; and whether eternal mind or eternal matter co-operated to produce them or not, we only know them as plain works of human art whose order and materials are alike changing before our eyes. We have no intention therefore to conjoin the spheres of Association and Absolute Truth, to go behind our relative truths and trace them back to Nature or to the Absolute. We therefore build our science consciously out of Human Associations, nothing else. Warned by the example of others who have tried to raise with the same materials Babels that have tumbled back on themselves, we know our limits; we intend to keep within them.

Yet within these limits all truths will not be of equal worth simply because they are relative. They will wear three faces: 1. Some will be antique theories or half-theories of past societies and their experiences. Feeble or hale they are not the children of the present. Trace their history. Compare them with their fellows of the present. They are only surviving; it is plain they are for death. 2. Others are the living reflections of living society. From associations almost personal they rise by tiers of generalization into *the* central truth of the living social organism, *the* principle which embodies or seems to embody its vitality. 3. Others are nascent truths, nascent beliefs radiating from present associations into an imaginary future.

Such being the three elements of social truth, the three kinds of social belief within any given social horizon, how shall we reach the true theory, the true θεωρία or *spectacle* of a given society, past or present? How shall we mark off associations and generalizations belonging to the given area? How reach the principle which sums up its characteristics? What are the tools with which we build particular experiences into that pyramid of generalization which we call our *theory* of a given social life?

I. The Comparative Method is one. In a given society you find a belief, say in inherited guilt. You have elsewhere found that belief to be a development of communal clan life. You infer that the given society moves or has moved through this social stage. You collect evidences from Language, Law, and Literature. Your proofs are complete. Finally you make your inference part of your mental picture, you make it part of your *theory* of that society.

II. But you are constructing a theory of *living* society. You want to distinguish those social theories or fragments of social theories which really harmonize with the living organism. You want to arrive through them at the principle which *now* holds the organism together. You divide the dead from the living theories; you call the former Survivals; and you find Survivals in social custom, in language, and in thought. You are clearing your social vision by the Methods of Comparison and *Survival*.

III. But you must do more. Your society may not be stationary. You may have reached a theory of your society *in equilibrio*. You may have distinguished a pale disc of your social theory, so to speak, of your present sphere of light and knowledge, the pale disc of survival. But your social theory is advancing. Like social life it refuses finality. To the pale disc passing away there corresponds another coming into being; it is the nascent beliefs, the nascent faiths of the future, just setting out on their progress from growth to decay. Your social abstractions, your social theory, the very principle of your social life, all contain this *ideal* element. If you have been forced to fill up your theories of past societies by the aid of imagination—if the most accurate acquaintance with the monuments of antiquity cannot relieve you from that necessity, you must prepare to employ the same aid in attempting to mentally combine the characteristics of *living* society. Suppose, for instance, you have examined every document of French, German or Italian history; suppose you have mentally tabulated every particular, every generalization of the nation's historical experience; yet you must still form by generalization your own theory of the people's development. You must imagine links where they have crumbled away, or have been but partially chronicled, or have never been written down at all. Inductions of popular thought confused and imperfect, deductions of popular thought more imperfect and more confused, you must imagine into clearness and precision. In a word, you must be constantly using Scientific Imagination. Theorize your own society and you will employ, consciously or unconsciously, the same method. Why? Because your effort in the one case is to *return upon*, in the other, to *anticipate* the genesis of social abstractions; and an element of all abstractions, popular or scientific, is that *imaginative*, that *ideal* element you consciously supply.

IV. In performing such analyses of evolution we shall take as our clue the concrete classifications of society. And why? Given a society; it has partially inherited, partially made for itself abstractions embodying theories more or less vague about its own being and the units of class and person it contains, theories it may be claiming universal application to all societies, claiming even to be Human Nature personified. Shall we content ourselves with leaving these abstractions unanalyzed? And by comparing and compounding them in that unanalyzed state, shall we raise an eclectic structure of our own on foundations never inspected? Or, shall we never rest until an anatomy at once Comparative and Historical has referred these popular abstractions to this or that concrete element of social life?

Take an example. Let us suppose that the abstract conception of Blood-Revenge has to be explained, not because it is any longer an element of social life, but because we are attempting to form our theory of a given society in which it is found, and that theory must be formed by reasoning differing *only in degree* from that which we apply to a living social body. If the method of explanation we adopt be Abstract Analysis, we cannot pass beyond such generalizations on the subject as certain social states have left us, and these we can only select after our arbitrary judgment. But let the method be Concrete Analysis. At once Arab *Thâr*, Hebrew *Ge'ullah*, or German *Wehrgeld* are traced to the social organism of the clan; at once we are on the way to construct a theory of communal ethics on the firm foundation of communal life.

Take another example. Let it be supposed that we belong to an age in which the phenomenon Credit no longer exists. The mass of literature on the subject bewilders us with countless theories; the entity Credit appears as metaphysical as the Schoolmen's essences. What is to be done? Just what the practical Economist of to-day does, viz., try to reach the concrete phenomena upon which the abstraction Credit depends. Thus the analysis of Social Science, the analysis of the Historical Method is the Concrete Analysis.

One other point and our methods are complete. Social Science is often assumed to start from the Individual, the Individual Mind. 'The Laws of Human Nature,' a commonplace in extensive circulation, are assumed to owe their existence to the One, not the Many. All Social Nature is regarded as the sum of the natures of the One. The hypothesis is that Social Life introduces no new factors of its own into Human Nature—in fact that Human Nature is Individual Human Nature. This hypothesis is readily disproved by showing that conceptions in which various ages have seen *the* characteristics of Human Nature have owed their origin to certain combinations of men in society.

Let me illustrate my meaning by two examples. The idea of the Hebrew Covenant or League (Berîth) is easily traced by Philology and Social Survivals to the common festivals of the clan. For at least two branches of the Semites that institution united clan to clan, tribe to tribe, city to city—' il ne faut pas perdre de vue que, dans les anciens

âges, ce qui faisait le lien de toute société, c' était un culte.'*
The conception of nationality under cover of eponymous kinship was its outgrowth in Israel. The language in which national kinship was expressed, and the exclusiveness of national morality implied bears the mark of that clan origin. The brotherhoods of these ancient communities lent their feelings and their languages to sustain and express sentiments of unity which their own ruin could alone have fostered. And when the decay of that nationality set in there rose from the ancient conception of brotherhood, once more revived, an ideal of Human Unity which passed from Palestine to Rome, and from Rome to the World. The village communes of a little Semite nation have left their being for ever idealized in the conception of Universal Brotherhood.

There is a companion conception which by an analogous process has passed from the concrete to the abstract, has risen from an origin no less humble, and embraces a complexity of interest no less wide. A group of hills was cultivated by hostile villages : three amalgamated, formed a city : uniformities in their customs became 'the law of the clans.' Their city grows into the head of a League, the centre of a City Federalism. And the common customs of the leaguered towns are assimilated to 'the law of the clans.' An abstraction is evolved: it is the *Jus Gentium* of Rome. In another land like attempts at fusion, at Federalism, are being made. Physical and other obstacles prevent success. The stage of City Autonomy is not passed. But the collision of small

* M. Coulanges " La Cité Antique," p. 166.

groups strikes out a vigorous social life which is reflected in Mind. The unity which society refuses is found in Nature, in Nature's Law. The idea is transferred to the steady but slower community. And the Greek Law of Nature idealizes the Jus Gentium into the Jus Naturale. We need not pursue the famous history of that conception traced by a famous Jurist, the theories which have circled round it, the revolutions to which it has been applied. As an example it has done its duty. I say again that conceptions in which various ages have seen *the* marks of Human Nature owe their origin to social conditions.

The existence, therefore, of a large body of thought traceable to social organization suffices to prove the possibility of a Social Science apart from Individual Human Nature, whatever that Individual Human Nature may be. In fact, the conception of Individual Human Nature as independent of inherited or acquired associations due to society is being every day circumscribed. Our social methods then are collective; they start from the group, from the Many, not from the One. They do so not solely because Individual Humanity is being traced back to evolution from a group, but also because the Humanity of our own day is far less the result of Individual than Social life, and tends increasingly to reflect the latter.

To finally answer our question, What are the tools with which we build experience into social theory, we have found that they are four—the Comparative Method, the Method of Survival, the Method of Scientific Imagination, and the Method of Concrete Analysis. I do not mean to say that this classification is by any means perfect, or that these methods do not intersect and overlap each other. But I adopt that classification as a sufficient description of the General Method under which these are to be ranged as species—that method which is to be associated not only with the past, but with the present and the future—the Historical Method.

What is the *raison d' être* of this Historical Method?

If I am not much mistaken it lies deep down in the genesis, the evolution of mind itself. But I must define my conception of that part of mind to which the Method is related. Mind may be an abstraction merely generalizing into a single expression a number of associations, or the term may be employed to denote the unknown mental cause or recipient of such associations. With the latter our method has nothing to do. But, as already said, I can see nothing to prevent a scientific treatment of associations as dependent on social relations alone. Any mental phenomena, therefore, which can be absolutely excluded from these limits do not come within the scope of the Historical Method. But although our method starts from the existence of some social group, the mind with which it deals will be the mind of each and every man *so far as it is compounded of such associations.* Whatever associations, therefore, of the individual mind can be shown historically to have derived their origin from social states, from the relation of the One to the Many, will belong to our science—nay more, whatever ideas can be analyzed back into such associations will also fall within our range.

Let us suppose a human being conscious of nothing but

single and apparently unrelated objects. Let him have no generalizations, no abstractions at all. Let him think entirely in the concrete. Can we imagine any effort to conjoin these isolated ideas without at least a vague conception of something *causing* the conjunction? We shall suppose, then, that the moment generalization begins the group of mentally associated ideas commences to throw a shadow of itself in this *implication of causality* whether consciously realized or not. This shadow-soul is next taken to be an entity quite independent of the substance, the association, and altogether superior to anything which that association includes. Then a question will arise, Is the entity within man or without man, or both? Whatever answers that question may evoke, the idea of *Universal Causation* will have been ultimately evolved by a series of widening and intersecting circles of generalization, each of which will contain the abstract implication of a known or unknown *cause*. Whether the Universal Cause finally reached be Chaos itself, that is, an entity corresponding to the abstract idea of universal confusion, or some entity corresponding to the abstract idea of universal order, such as God, the idea itself will be the sum of these smaller circles of causation implied in the progress of generalization. I do not of course pretend that this hypothetical progress represents the historical evolution of thought, nor do I suppose that we possess the requisite materials for such a history. But since I believe the Historical Method to be nothing but the Historical Reversal of Social and Mental Evolution, the hypothesis thus briefly sketched seems best to indicate the relation which I conceive to subsist between the Historical Method and such evolution. That relation I shall now attempt to illustrate.

I. The Comparative Method is one of construction as well as destruction. Thus, a number of general ideas in a given society are constructed by its foremost intellects into a theory of that society's being. It may be unhistorical. It may confuse the most alien conceptions. The edifice finally reared may be the most astounding piece of motley architecture destined to delight the analytic soul of the future historian. Still it is a social theory, and, moreover, a social theory formed by the Comparative Method, so far as it went. Let in a flood of new lights, of cross-lights upon that society's history. Let a kindred but elder social group be disentombed. Compare their respective customs, their languages, their thought. From many another social history collect analogies. And, armed with superior knowledge, attack once more the well-known records of the unhistorical theorists. Why, you find yourself upon a hill. You see the life of the social group forming its unhistorical abstractions before your eyes. You correct their popular theories, you correct the theories of their religious scientists, you give historical order to unhistorical confusion, and you do all simply with a larger, a keener instrument of *Comparison*.

But you are a Jurist, let us suppose, a Roman Jurist. Boldly you open your teaching with the declaration that the laws of every people 'are partly peculiar to itself, partly belong to all mankind,' and that 'the rules prescribed by *Natural Reason* (*Ratio Naturalis*) *for all* are observed by all nations alike.' 'Though every system of law has its specific and characteristic differences,' chimes in the cautious Englishman at a distance, 'there are principles, notions, and distinctions common to various systems, and forming analogies or likenesses by which such systems are allied.' In the lapse of time the 'Natural Reason' has been gently put aside. Why? Because the range of Comparative Knowledge has widened. Because that expansion has proved that 'Natural Reason' is a relative term. Because the resemblance of general principles has been found to depend on the resemblance of social life. Because the Mental Evolution has been found to depend in no small degree on the Social.

It is needless to multiply examples in order to show the relation of Conscious Comparison to Mental Evolution, the theories it is perpetually constructing in the minds of each and all, the theories which by a display of glaring contradictions it as perpetually destroys. We shall admit, then, that the Comparative Method consciously or unconsciously employed, in clumsy or scientific hands, is a part of Mental Evolution, and varies in value with the degree that evolution has reached.

II. A single survival, like the geologist's perched block, often marks the trail of a whole mental glacier that has flowed and melted noiselessly away. Thus the literature of a cultured nation contains a reference to the belief of its ancestors in an ancient and universal flood. In that reference the historical and comparative scientist sees a fragment of the Archaic Physics which explained the phenomenon rain as the outpouring of an ocean above the sky, above the firmament, which explained the mysterious mountain-spring by a likewise mysterious communication with some under-world ocean, and which expresses its theory of the origin of rivers as due to such oceanic circulation in language which has been actually applied to the atmospheric circulation of modern science.

Many a survival crops out from language itself. Thus for a certain Semitic people the sun does not 'rise' or 'set'; he 'goes forth,' he 'comes in.' And from such a survival in speech we might mentally pass back to the childish imagination that pictured the sun-god going forth to his work like man, and like man coming home to his rest. We call that a childish imagination, and no doubt there were men in that ancient people who regarded it not merely as childish but wicked. Yet as often as we speak of the 'rising' and the 'setting' sun we must remember that we, too, must often speak in myth.

It is true that survivals in thought and speech and custom have often proved the greatest obstacles to mental clearness, and indeed must continue to do so until their proper place in social and mental evolution is discovered. Strangely out of place, they may be observed built up in many a popular theory of social life. And yet it is by their aid that the scientist may now-a-days bridge over wide gaps in history. Now, what is the cause of these survivals? They are nothing absolute, they are relative to the progress of the social organism, of the social mind, of the individual mind. What is a *Survival* in the estimation of the scientist is nothing but plain common sense for a less developed intellect. What is the highest reason in one age is but *superannuated* reason in another. Thus the idea of inherited guilt has survived from the age of clan ethics, from the liabilities of the fourth and fifth generation, and, like other fragments of communal ethics, is still a favourite material in popular morality. The survival, then, is a piece of thought, a piece of language, or a piece of social life carried out of the associations which produced it into others. And while it owes its origin no less than its decay to associations, its recognition as a *Survival* implies *the conscious Comparison and Contrast* of different historical stages of Mental Evolution. I say, then, that the Method of Survival, like the Comparative Method, is a part of Mental Evolution.

III. The Method of Historical Analysis is quite transparently mental, and exposes the very Relativity of Reasoning itself. You have analyzed your mental operations, let us suppose. You have taken your reasoning to pieces. You have labelled every part of its improved machinery—this, Induction; that, Deduction. And you have thrown into a dark corner a quantity of oldfashioned lumber, over which you have written the ominous word 'Fallacy.' Try to apply that new machinery universally; try to carry it beyond the circle of intellect developed like your own, and you cease to be understood. Your most brilliant achievements only suggest some latent trick. Why is this? I shall try to illustrate the reason.

A nation—it is a 'natio,' merely a big clan—is fused into unity. Its tongue, the common product of a mass of barbarous groups, is gradually developed into a magnificent organ of speech, upon which the poets, the orators, the philosophers of a polished age perform their marvellous symphonies of thought and language. Who has watched that silent growth ? Who *knows* the marks of that barbarous origin ? At last the grammarian, proverbially dryest of mortals, takes the great instrument to pieces and classes its wonderful notes as verbs and nouns and particles. But if he tries to carry that analysis indefinitely backwards, he ceases to be true, he ceases to be historic, his noun and verb and particle are carried into an age before their historic birth.

And this is why your admirable logic loses its effect beyond definite limits. You address living men, it is true; you even address them in their own tongue; but their mental development may be far behind yours, and you must translate your thoughts into their mental analysis or change their mental analysis into your own.

Historical Analysis, therefore, is far from being a monopoly of past history; it is full of import for the present; it is, as the people say, practical—eminently practical. Go into our Courts of Justice, and what do you find ? Judicial analyses of motives, of whole trains of thought, from actions or words, from even one significant action or word. What tacit assumption underlies these analyses ? Why, that trained intelligence may fill up gaps in thought just as the historian interprets his survivals, that trained intelligence may know more of another's thought than he has chosen to express, nay, more than even he himself has known. Stewart, criticising a passage in Hobbes's *Leviathan*, in which an example of association is given, remarks that the person in whose mind the process had taken place might have been unable to trace the connexion of his own thoughts, while men like Hobbes, accustomed to back upon the genesis of their own ideas, could readily do so. And there are collective as well as individual incapacities of attending to sensations and ideas which, as the Reviewer of Hamilton says, 'once entered into trains of thought,' and both incapacities are the work of association. If, therefore, mental automatism (to use Hartley's expression) is characteristic of those innumerable little spheres of individual associations which intersect each other with bewildering intricacy, its effects will be seen in past and present theories of society, philosophic as well as popular; and the revelation of that mental automatism by the aid of concrete social phenomena is the function of Historical Analysis in theorizing states of society, whether past or present. The Historical Method of Analysis is therefore an interpretation of Mental Evolution.

A human being alone, without Language, without Literature, without Religion, without Morality, without Law—strip man of the associations he owes to society, and that is the savage nakedness in which he stands. You may call him a noble savage if you will. Your disgust at existing social abuses may dress him out in all the virtues whose absence you now deplore. But however piquant your contrast, your 'Natural' man is a mere figment, an *Unnatural* figment; it is the πολιτικὸν ζῷον, it is the being whose vices and virtues affect and are affected by the family, the society, that is the true man, the historic man. Genius or instinct, all the wonderful unexplained things of Sculpture and Music, of Poetry and Painting, who will find, who will imagine them apart from social life? I am far from saying that every mental and manual aptitude of man has yet been traced to his social relations, or that we shall ever dig far down into that vast mass of buried social life which could alone enable us to confirm our conjectures. I am as far from saying that if this were possible, if it were done, the gloomy inferences of dogmatic Materialism would by any means follow. The Historical Method is collective, it starts from the group, the associations of the group, but it is far from being materialistic, and that vast evolution of thought and speech and action, over which it delights to range, confirms rather than impairs the inscrutable dignity of the unknown mental eye, which sees so close to itself and to such immense distances the multitudinous shapes of mental growth and decay. I say, then, that the Historical Method starts from social life, and deals with the evolution that life affords, both in the One and in the Many; but I deny that it is materialistic.

IV. There is a very old comparison of social life to a river. If we imagine each and every drop of that river moving at rates of progress differing in infinitesimal degrees, from the gliding friction along the banks to the swiftest rush of the central stream; if, moreover, we refuse to carry back indefinitely our *present* vision or theory of the broad flood, if we do not forget the innumerable tributaries which from time to time must have fallen in—nay, if we can picture the great river itself frittered away into countless rivulets whose claim to priority we cannot decide, then I say, if that be our vision of social life, we are close to the reason of Historical Method.

Our social progress and its mental counterpart are *not uniform ;* for each social unit, for each individual unit, the rate of that progress is *constantly varying.* *That* is the secret of the Historical Method, its Survivals, its Comparisons. For how does the relativity of social progress affect us ? A thinker sifts his associations, tests them by concrete analysis, at last theorizes them into an explanation of *his own* origin and destiny. But he is only one drop in the social stream, and his associations impinge on the motions of many other like drops. If he is to think at all, therefore, his theory must widen into a theory of *human* origin and destiny. Yet he cannot rest content with a vision of what has merely *been;* he seeks to find what *made* it be. He may have mentally followed back the origin of society into the countless rivulets from which it has taken rise, but he feels constrained to go *farther.* On the wings of fancy he passes from the rivulets to the rain-clouds, from earth to heaven, and in that lofty atmosphere throws the reins to his Imagination. It is the Historical Method which enables us to retrace that progress step by step, and to pause before we pass from the Known to the Unknown. Under that guidance, Imagination Scientifically controlled ceases to be the master, the Ariel of Science finds his Prospero, and obeys his limits.

Is it necessary to point out the relation of Imagination to the Evolution of Thought ? Why, the whole history of thought is also *its* history. Every popular, every scientific theory worth mentioning displays its handiwork for weakness or for strength ; the very idea of *Mental,* of *Social Evolution* is to be reckoned among its creatures.

What is Scientific Hypothesis? With a strange freedom it ranges through time and space—now in the almost poetical vision of rippling waves of light, now in the gigantic periods of geological time. What is it but Imagination, controlled, systematized, supported on probabilities, but still Imagination? By its aid man advances into the unknown, be it a step or be it far, and leaves the limits of legitimate reason. By its aid he stands by the unseen workings of Nature and of Mind, fills in the gaps that were otherwise unexplained, and creates within and without himself a symmetrical universe of law and order. Call it by as dignified a name as you please, Hypothesis is no monopoly of modern science, of modern generalization. Trace its history, trace it backwards, and it slowly widens into the uncontrolled Imagination of Primitive Mind. What is true of all other parts of the Historical Method is, therefore, also true of Scientific Imagination; it is part of Mental Evolution. I repeat that the Historical Method has its roots deep down in the development of mind itself.

But the question remains, What is this ideal, this will-o'-the-wisp element in Generalization against which we must be perpetually on guard? I do not say that it has always been so in the same degree. I am far from saying that it has always been consciously realized, but I cannot help regarding that element as at bottom the notion of *Causation*. Just as the notion of Causation underlies all Scientific Induction, so it seems to underlie all Popular Induction. I believe that an historical examination of Generalization, marking as far as possible the narrow limits which at first separate it from the Concrete and Particular, following its expansion by the aid of Philological evidences, and tracing its growth into Abstractions superior to the phenomena out of which they arose, will ultimately confirm this conjecture. And whatever opinion we adopt on this notion of Causation, it must settle our philosophy. We shall from that moment stand on this side or that in the battle of the Absolute, or withdraw to the limited yet ample field of Relative Truth. For if our notion of Cause passes behind relations into an entity, then the progress of Generalization will of necessity imply a goal of Absolute Truth, whether in Mind or Matter. It was on this account that I laid down the principle that Social Science and the Historical Method deal with nothing but Relative Truths. Otherwise it would be necessary to find some causal entity which forces society into this or that framework; and, even though the relation between Mind and that framework might be still admitted, we should be called upon to see through both into the workings of the superior entity beyond. We have disclaimed ability to do so; we have strictly limited the range of our Science and its Method. But it will be well to realize more fully what that disclaimer and that limitation mean. I shall attempt to briefly realize their meaning in three branches of Social Science, in Ethics, in Jurisprudence, and in Political Economy.

CHAPTER II.

THE HISTORICAL METHOD IN ETHICS.

THE first practical inquiry in Ethics, as in most Sciences, must be, What is its existing State, and how was it reached? Without an accurate answer to this question our science will remain a jumble of confusion, and its progress, if it makes any progress, will be mere inert drifting. The practical value of an Ethical System must depend upon its relation to social life. It is true that the uneven Mental and Social development of the units composing a given society will carry along many a fragment of Ethical systems which rose to the surface far away up-stream. But that is the very reason why their origin should be carefully chronicled, and their real value suspiciously tested. If, therefore, the Ethical beliefs of totally different social conditions are to be deliberately confounded, no matter how mutually repellent, no matter how unsuited to living society, there can be nothing but a minimized chance of success resulting, not from, but in spite of, the method employed. Historical truth is in such a case directly excluded by the bare hypothesis. A Comparative Jurist starts with the admission (for him a truism) that 'nothing is more dangerous than a partial repeal of legal principles which leaves other principles, their logical antecedents or consequences, still subsisting, or an ill-considered reform which leaves mingled in hopeless confusion enactments of different origin and contradictory nature.' An Economist must be ready to admit a like Relativity under penalties which the history of his science only too deplorably exemplifies. In Ethics, if in any social science, this recognition of Historical Relativity is desirable; yet in Ethics, more than in any other social science, this relativity is discarded. The mere development of Ethical generalization going on almost before our eyes—the Ethics of new International relations, of new Credit relations, for example—ought to correct this unhistoric attitude of the Moral Scientist. The very manner of the development of Ethical generalizations ought to correct him. They rise after a fashion very like, only much worse, than that of Case-made Law. Very like, because they are popular findings upon sets of conditions compared with uncertain principles uncertainly realized. Much worse, because they have been drawn, in language the most threadbare and obscure, and in a happy-go-lucky way have been set down *without the circumstances they once represented*. Accordingly it is the task of the historical moralist to recover those circumstances, and to scientifically test the value of those popular inductions as expressed in their own vague way; to determine the applicability of Archaic Ethics to living Society; and finally to construct a sound Ethical theory, an Ethical theory historically true, by the aid, and in the place of, the confused popular substitutes.

But the Ethical Scientist is popularly expected to do more,

much more than this. We can imagine an able lawyer making tolerably good work with a volume of obscure and contradictory principles unaccompanied by the concrete cases from which they had been drawn. But if it were his duty not only to bring his own case within these principles, but also to frame a rule capable of including all the old contradictions as well as his own new formula, the task might well be believed to surpass his or any other man's honest ability. Yet this is the very task with which, as a matter of course, the Ethical Scientists have saddled themselves. Everyone knows how they have borne the burden. Everyone knows the thorough disrepute into which the whole study, a most practical study, had fallen before the first appearance of Historical and Comparative treatment. Even at the present moment some of the contempt which the old method, or rather absence of method, deserved, affects indirectly the entire Science. In fact, it might almost be asked, Where is the Science? The rise of a body of distinctly *Ethical* principles has been prevented. Some of these are the prescriptive possession of the Jurist, some of the Economist; and while the Moralist has been snoring over his fancied universal treasure of all ages' good things, almost everything of practical value has come into new hands. Nor will he gain much by dressing up what remains in a fantastic transcendental garb no longer understood by living society. There may be much to alarm; but an imitation of the pompous tricks of all decaying power is not the way to re-establish an Ethical Science. Does the sacred architect of our Ethical Beliefs offer glimpses of a strange origin, an origin far stranger than the Christian

Church that scarcely conceals in its form the structure of the heathen law-court? Will others retire because our timid inspection retires? Will others be mute because, with our fingers on our lips, we are prepared to imitate the gloomy multitude in Beckford's romance, and pass and repass each other in eternal silence? No. If the science of Ethics is to possess any living force at all, we must boldly, though reverently, separate the dead from the living; we must formulate an Ethical Theory suited to our own social conditions; we must, for practical valuation, refer all other Ethical conceptions to that standard, and we must admit that in Ethics, as in every other branch of human thought, we have found decay as well as growth—

> 'Many a fallen old divinity
> Wandering in vain about bewildered shores.'

The first step, then, for the practical Moralist must be to recover what his own supineness has lost; and the only claim to such recovery likely to be admitted must rest on a sweeping use of the Historical Method which will reveal the Relative and Unabsolute character of his science, as of all social sciences, the true relative values of archaic and modern morality, and the pressing need of an Ethical Science accurately formulating its historical, including in that term both practical and speculative, phenomena. Thus, instead of dragging on an effete Law of Nature and like worn-out abstractions as convenient receptacles for sundry moralities—instead of creating Moral Senses and other weak reproductions of material organisms, we shall set out in Moral Science with the conviction that our materials are

Relative and not Absolute, that our highest moral ideals must partake of the same character, and that we shall have made at least one step towards a practical science of morality, if we give up the practice of appealing to conceptions which now-a-days owe more to imagination than the associations of life. 'The moment we enter on the comparison of savage and civilised Ethics,' says Mr. Tylor, 'there parts and falls away before our eyes a thick curtain which has shut in the view of whole schools of moralists, and that for many ages. When in the seventeenth century Locke took up fragments of ethnographic evidence from the meagre store then available, he could hurl them with crushing force against the school of intuitive moralists. He appeals to any who have been but moderately conversant with the history of mankind, and looked beyond the smoke of their own chimneys, to say whether nature has stamped those *universal principles* on the minds of barbarians who, with public approbation or allowance, expose or bury alive, or eat their childern, or kill their aged parents, or cast out the dying to perish by cold and hunger or to be torn by wild beasts.' Systems of Ethics more or less consciously expressed, more or less perfect in their day have, whether we know or care to know it, vanished in the progress of Society and Mind. Systems of Ethics, whether we see or care to see it, are gliding from amongst us at this moment, while others with strange faces are growing familiar by the slowness of their approach. A question, the answer to which must make the pivot of our Ethical System, is whether we shall admit such facts and act upon the admittance, or shut our eyes to them.

It is a question of the deepest social meaning. I think I am not exaggerating its importance when I say that the future fate of society depends upon the way in which that question is solved. We cannot lapse with impunity into moral antiquities. We cannot accept as Absolute Truth ideas of right and wrong based upon clan responsibility, and be ready next moment to analyze recondite elements of Intention. We cannot admit as Eternal Truths the strange and terrible sanctions of such an archaic system, and the next moment minutely proportion punishment to offence or deterrent effect. The contrast is too conscious. The contradiction is too glaring. If we think at all, we must recognize the survival. But it is precisely when we do not think at all that the danger is greatest. Not five men in every hundred, perhaps nothing like so many, take the trouble to consciously examine their Ethical conceptions, to compare, to contrast them. They are far from being able to say what is or what is not contradictory in them. Their moral world is at best a confused jumble of moral survivals supported by early associations, attempts to practically apply these, and more or less evident collisions between these attempts and practical principles vaguely understood and vaguely valued. If the effects of this confusion did not extend beyond depreciating the moral worth of Intention, or introducing through the conception of inherited sin a species of Fatalism, or discouraging personal responsibility and the cultivation of self-control by attributing more or less of men's actions to external agency, the consequences might still be regarded as sufficiently serious. But there are others much more serious. There is a direct tendency to depreciate the value of all morality, If a man has been taught to regard such principles as *divine elements in his moral nature*—for that is the phrase—the reduction of their divinity by Historical Analysis to the common light of human life, to the plain reflection of social conditions, may depreciate, in his eyes, the worth of *all* morality. Senseless and impractical, that inference would deny the value of morality because it is found to be Relative, as if the value of *everything human* is not Relative, as if Absolute Truth, were it to walk before our eyes, would not of necessity be clothed in that Relativity. But senseless and impractical as that inference would be, it is, so far as it goes, an argument—an argument for the unhistorical, the *uninquiring*, defenders of Archaic Ethics. But it is an argument which destroys itself, for it is based on that power of association which it refuses to historically question. Moreover, the real issue has been already settled in the Political and Economic fields, viz. whether an abuse is to shelter itself behind the abuses it has begotten. Sooner or later there will come in Ethics the same unqualified negative that question has elsewhere received.

And the employment of the Historical Method in Ethics is *for the soundest interests of society*. Let us prove that point. The periods at which moral conceptions are sure to be subjected to criticism are precisely those at which it is most dangerous that they should be so subjected. Hence it often happens in times of social revolution, or rapid transition, that the most antiquated morality commands unquestioning obedience, while that upon which the very *existence* of the living society depends can gain but scanty courtesy, or is almost openly repudiated. Such is the result of allowing the real ratio of moral values to be unhistorically inverted. Given two Land-Systems based respectively on Competition and Custom, under which will the moral obligations of Contract be of greatest practical value? What is the relative value of Credit and its morality in England compared with India, or in England of to-day compared with England of three centuries back? Yet while I write, how many are breaking through obligations of Contract and Credit who would shudder to repudiate belief in Inherited Sin? How many do not act with them, yet think with them, and place misunderstood and obsolete morality far above that which *binds our very society together?* Such men are unconsciously acting or thinking as if all morality were nothing but *masses of survivals;* as if the present had no morality for itself, and any collapse of the old must leave a moral blank. I say that such thinking, if it is not historically corrected, will one day be the ruin of our society. I repeat, therefore, that the honest use of the Historical Method in Ethics is for the soundest social interests.

How far have the principles of the Historical Method been applied in recent Ethical systems? To answer this question let us briefly examine Utilitarianism, accepting Mr. Mill's exposition as the clearest statement of its latest form.

There is one sentence in Mr. Mill's essay which, perhaps unconsciously, displays his stand-point in a clear light. 'Happiness,' he says, 'is *not an abstract idea, but a concrete whole.*' Happiness is accordingly an entity, consisting of all and every element of Individual and Social pleasure, without any attempt to distinguish their historical relativity to Social and Individual conditions. The mental process exemplified in Mr. Mill's statement of Utilitarianism has been often illustrated by the generalizations in which different stages of society have seen abstractions superior to and supplementing their moral phenomena, only that Mr. Mill's generalization professes to be *peculiarly concrete*, whereas the others have been as a rule *peculiarly abstract*. The early Semitic and Greek thinkers, who gathered up the confused elements of a material world stocked with all manner of deities into the concrete generalization called Chaos, did as Mr. Mill does. But is the generalization in either case concrete because it is merely thought of as such? I think not. I think that in the case of the early philosophers the concrete attitude was assumed because thinking in the abstract was not yet fully developed; because, in fact, the mind required a concrete prop to support its abstractions. In Mr. Mill's case, the concrete form of his general idea seems to me a mere objective idealism—a makeshift for avoiding *the imaginary element*, which I conceive to exist of necessity in every generalization, to consist in an implication of causality, and to be exposed by the Inductive and Deductive process in thinking, *i.e.* by the Analysis of Mental Evolution. It is no objection to Mr. Mill's Ethical theory or generalization that it contains this imaginative element; if it did not, if it were purely concrete, it would not be a generalization at all. And even if all generalization does not imply imagination, it is certainly the aim of a moral theory partially to supply an ideal, an imaginative standard, which is the very reason why each of the moral generalizations or theories thrust into prominence by Social Evolution has displayed a tendency to usurp the whole field of Ethics, and augmented the vagueness of its own boundaries by a temporary invasion of all its neighbours. Nothing has contributed more to Ethical stationariness than this *postulation of universality* for every prominent moral conception in turn. What would have been the progress of the Physical Sciences had every generalization claimed universality, and had this claim supported by unanalyzed associations been allowed by scientific acquiescence? It is Mr. Mill's uncertain attitude on this subject which is the gravest objection to his Moral Philosophy. For it was the duty of an Ethical inquirer, an Ethical *historian*, to direct attention to the confusing characteristic of Moral Philosophy just noted. It was still more his duty to exemplify his warning by the most careful avoidance of any such claim to universality in his own theory, and to cut away from that theory any others, no matter how useful or popular, which advanced the same claim. The simplest way of doing this would have been, to have proved from history, and allowed in his own theory the necessarily factitious or imaginative nature of any universal moral standard; to have admitted that his own theory, in order to contain a standard at all, in order even to be a generalization at all, must include this imaginative element, must pass beyond facts and beyond the concrete; that this theory must be historically impossible under certain past, and dependent for its approximate truth on certain present, social conditions;

that it is sure to be altered more or less rapidly with social progress; yet that in its author's opinion it most aptly expresses and directs the Ethics of our day, and best supplies an Ethical want of all societies capable of reflection, viz. a defined standard of human action.

This is exactly what Mr. Mill has *not* done. While the whole tone of his own Philosophy is against our knowledge of Absolute Truth—not of course against its existence, which would be negative absolutism within the limits of associations, *i. e.* a contradiction in terms—he displays a strange hankering after absoluteness in Ethics. He writes as if it were the duty of the moralist to formulate a principle capable of including every standard of Morals, from which popular approval has not yet been *definitely* withdrawn, a principle applicable, by some inherent virtue, to all conditions, to all persons, to all times, to all places. That Mr. Mill was far from despairing of such a principle may be inferred from his effort to prove Happiness (as extended in its connotation by himself) *the* sole criterion of morality. He has thus placed himself in the remarkable position of an associationist, manufacturing out of associations an Absolute Ethical criterion, instead of finding in the Historical Evolution of Society and Mind the impossibility of such criteria, and pointing to the search for them as itself in the course of becoming a mental survival. In the only case where he seems to be on the verge of employing the Historical Method in his essay, his verbal analysis of Justice does not lead him to ask why it is that an appeal to language and the social state reflected by language is so needful in the obscure terminology of Ethics. Inadvertences like these are, in my opinion, the necessary result of Mr. Mill's failure to understand the relation between the Association Philosophy and the Historical Method. This method is, to my mind, the complement of that philosophy. By their co-operation we are entering on an era of mind when it will no longer be possible to despise or deify its furniture simply as of known or mysterious making. This I take to be the practical meaning of that Revolution in Philosophy which the Historical Method, even as at present clumsily handled, is not slowly effecting. It is this Revolution which will render innocuous the recognition of the factitious nature of universal moral standards. And it is this Revolution which I must believe to have been inadequately expressed in the Ethical, and indeed all the works of Mr. Mill. I do not, therefore, regard Mr. Mill's Ethical system, or indeed any other form of Utilitarianism, as an example of the Historical Method applied to Moral Science. We shall now take a hurried glance at a more advanced system than that of Mr. Mill, the *Ethical Data* of Mr. Herbert Spencer. The question for us is, Are these Ethical Data examples of the Historical Method?

There are three Great Problems of Ethics to which the most diverse answers have been given : What is the best end or aim of Individual life? What is the best end or aim of Social life? Are these ends or aims identical? All the greatest questions of Ethics have sought directly or indirectly to solve these three problems. What idea, for example, underlies the variously expressed conceptions that Virtue and

Knowlege are one, that the Good Citizen and the Good Man are one? The idea that the apparent hostility of Individual and Social interests is not a *real* hostility, that knowledge will dispel the false show, and that the ideal ends of Social and Individual life are, if not identical, at least harmonious. What but the same idea underlies the variously expressed conception that the Conscience, the moral Self-Knowledge, of the One and the Many are the same, or at least in harmony? The ideal harmony of Social and Individual Mind has left its marks on all popular and scientific morality, and the meaning of that ideal is simply this: that man cannot contemplate without pain an apparent conflict between the ends or the means of knowing the ends of Social and Individual life. Therefore it is that, with anxious care, he sorts out the principles of conduct which seem most general, least peculiar to this or that man, least peculiar to this or that society. Therefore it is that he calls these principles Eternal, Immutable, the Dictates of Right Reason, the Mandates of Natural Law. For are not the Right Reason, the Natural Reason of the One, and the Rational Nature, the Natural Reason of the Many, harmonious? And are not they both harmonious with our conceptions of God? 'Jus Naturale,' says Grotius, 'est *dictatum rectae rationis*, indicans actui alicui, ex ejus convenientiâ aut disconvenientiâ *cum ipsâ Naturâ Rationali et Sociali*, inesse moralem turpitudinem aut necessitatem moralem, ac *consequenter ab Auctore Naturae Deo* talem actum aut vetari aut praecipi.' It is thus that Intuition in many ages has linked the most commanding generalizations of morality with an assumed Harmony of Social and Individual Consciences and Interests, and through that Natural Human Harmony with the Great Abstraction of Harmony Himself.

What, on the other hand, is the meaning of all that Ethical thought which from various stand-points judges the distinctions of morality by the principle of Sympathy and Antipathy, as Mr. Bentham says? What but the recognition of the apparent conflict between the morality of the One and the Many and the necessity of effecting even the most artificial reconciliation. 'One man says, he has a thing made on purpose to tell him what is right and what wrong, and that it is called a Moral Sense; and then he goes to work at his ease and says, such a thing is right and such a thing is wrong—Why? "because my Moral Sense tells me it is."' Why is it that this Moral Sense must be shared with all mankind, even with the certainty of being found so unhistorical and false when such an extension is attempted? Why does another tell you that his Common Sense 'is possessed by all mankind; the sense of those whose sense is not the same as his being struck out of the account as not worth taking'? Why does another say that 'all good and wise men *understand* moral distinctions as he does'? In fact, after all Mr. Bentham's criticism, what does his own dogma intend to do? The 'pretended systems' of morals are trying to answer the very same Problems, and, as we shall see in our next Chapter, their answers have been hardly more artificial, hardly less historical than Mr. Bentham's own. I shall now proceed to ask whether those Problems have been historically treated by Mr. Spencer.

In a recent article of the *Contemporary Review*, Mr. Goldwin Smith has published a critique, mainly dealing with Mr. Herbert Spencer's *Data of Ethics,* in which he says that 'the philosophers of the Ultra-Evolutionary School put out of sight in the scientific sweep of their Social Theories two commonplace facts—individuality and death.' With this opinion I fully concur, but I would explain the fact differently. It seems to me that neither the critic nor the philosophic school he criticises have restricted their Ethics to the limits of the Relative, the Unabsolute; and yet the need of this restriction is the very lesson of those Myths and Survivals between which, according to Mr. Goldwin Smith, 'there will soon be no room left for any *natural* belief.' I italicise the word 'natural,' for what is a *natural* belief? It is just this very question which underlies the innumerable attempts to harmonize the Ethics of the One and the Many, and it is the answer we give to this question which will carry our philosophy away into the Absolute or confine it to the Relative. Is a 'natural' belief one which the constitution of our Individual Mind forces on us? Then, unless we assume that this Individual *Nature* is identical with Social *Nature,* what do we reach but countless little spheres of Individual Nature unconnected, repellent, unharmonious? We must go deeper, then, than Individual Nature; we must find something less changing and uncertain. If that something is the Nature of Society in the sense of the most general principles of that Society's particular beliefs, or if, extending the conception to the whole Human Species, that something is the Nature of the Species in the sense of the most general principles its beliefs and experience have built up, then the very Relativity and Unabsoluteness of such principles preclude any but a Limited and Relative Moral Philosophy, and forbid the confusion of the Relative with the Absolute. But if you are not content to stop here, if you are determined to unite Human Nature, the sum of Individual Human Harmonies, with the conception of God or Matter as the sum of Universal Harmonies—if you are determined to see in Human Nature and its Individual parts a fragment or fragments of Eternal Mind or of Eternal Matter, then your 'Natural' beliefs are Absolute beliefs, and as such they do not fall within the limits of the Historical Method. Just as there are beliefs expressing the relations of the One to the Many, so there are beliefs expressing those of the One to external nature or to his own bodily structure. But to trace these beliefs into an Absolute Matter or Mind is, from the historical point of view, to throw indefinitely backwards in time or space or beyond them the inherent *petitio principii* of reasoning—universality from particularity—and to scientifically repeat the process of early thought upon a grand scale, viz., the projection of the Relative into the Absolute. I say again, therefore, that with the hypothetical eternities of Mind or Matter the Historical Method, as I conceive it, has nothing to do; the beliefs and theories with which it deals are Relative, Limited, Uneternal, Mutable, and the Human Nature with which it deals is the same.

How have we reached this recognition of Relativity? I shall attempt to answer this question because, as it seems to me, the answer will show why it is that Historical Evolution appears, as Mr. Goldwin Smith says, to overlook a commonplace like Individuality. How, then, have we reached that recognition of Relativity? Aided by all the modern improvements of increased communication and knowledge, we have looked around us, compared, contrasted, analyzed. We have found peoples of lower civilisation judging moral questions by other standards than our own, yet such standards as their Social and Individual conditions plainly supplied. We have followed up the history of our own theories on the same subject, and we have found them to be partially built out of fragments which have come down to us from the remotest antiquity, and which, like the rude theories of living barbarism, once aptly reflected the social conditions under which they arose. Are we to draw the hasty and absurd inference that there is no Truth, no Absolute Truth, from the existence of that Relativity? Are we to imitate the Greek Sophist, and, with far ampler securities for correctness, allow ourselves to be confused by the phenomena which on a far narrower field of experience confused him? The autonomous cities of Hellas had found in their laws the standards of Absolute Truth, and the Public Opinion of each petty commonwealth had ascribed to its own customs an authority divine and eternal. And as the Sophist in his search for free speech and free thought passed from city to city, the comparison of these standards forced itself on his attention, and the contrast of their contradictions led him to infer the non-existence of Absolute Truth. That inference was a contradiction in terms; it passed beyond the inherent *petitio principii* in reasoning; it passed beyond the universal conclusion from particular premises; it actually negatived the possibilities of the Absolute and Unknown by the most narrow experiences of the Relative and the Known. Such was the first famous example of the use of that Comparative Method whose end and limits the thinkers of to-day are slowly, very slowly realizing. It is plain that unless we are prepared to be even more illogical than the Sophist, we shall not draw his inference from the vast mass of Comparative materials which now lies at our disposal.

I said that the manner in which our recognition of Relativity has been forced on us by Conscious Contrast would explain the objection of Mr. Herbert Spencer's critic in the *Contemporary*, the objection that the Evolutionary thinking appears to ignore such common-places as Individuality and Death. I shall now attempt to remove that objection, and shall then briefly examine the Ethical System which Mr. Goldwin Smith's criticism had particularly in view. The mere progress of Generalization, if I am right in regarding that progress as the merging of smaller into larger circles of Generalization through the idea of Causation consciously or unconsciously presented, creates a number of conceptions which possess, so to speak, two faces. As facing the Limited, the Relative, they focus a number of such phenomena in one expression, one Generalization, one Centre of Causality. As facing the Unlimited, the Imaginary—using that term without the association of unreality—the Absolute, these generalizations are like lanterns throwing forward the reflection of their limited light into the darkness of the Unknown, and acquiring from the very impenetrability of that darkness an unreal value. No matter how magnificent such generalisations may be, we shall find that they carry us no distance at all into the Unknown, and nothing has done more melancholy work in thought than the sad recognition of the fact that some supposed and even glorious knowledge of the Absolute was after all only a reflection of the Relative. It is by the Historical Method that such reflections have been traced back to their plain realities. But it is not generalizations alone that have this double aspect. There are concrete facts as well as sets of concrete phenomena which stand in such close proximity to the Unknown as to have become invested with its awful dignity. Such facts are those of man's Birth, Individuality, and Death. No one needs to be reminded of the philosophic or popular imagination which has clothed these three in transfigurations splendid or terrible. But it must again be repeated, that whatever the relation of such facts to the Absolute may be, with those relations the Historical Method has nothing to do. If, therefore, an Ethical Philosophy of the Relative and Unabsolute exists, it is not logical to challenge its value because it refuses to pass beyond its own defined limits. But to secure that defence no attempt must have been made to transcend those limits; the philosophy in question must not only have recognized the principle of Relativity as its *own* principle, but must have formed its whole theory upon that recognition. Does the Ethical Philosophy of Mr. Herbert Spencer contain any attempt to transcend those limits, and does it therefore maintain or lose its claim to that defence?

We have found that the fundamental problems in Ethics

are three : What is the end of Individual Life ? What is the end of Social Life ? Are these ends Identical ? What are Mr. Herbert Spencer's answers to these problems ? As far as direct statement and direct answer are concerned, Mr. Spencer does not seem to be much clearer than Mr. Bentham. I cannot find any plain statement or any plain solution of the three problems between the covers of the *Data of Ethics*. But I have found quite enought to show that the real problems discussed are not different from these, and *to a certain degree* are treated historically. What then is the unhistorical element, for I have intimated my belief that the essay does contain such an element ?

There seems to be an idea prevalent among materialistic thinkers that Physical Science is destined to reconcile the apparent conflict of Social and Individual Ethics, and that the Mental Evolution of the Individual as analyzed by Physiology will some day afford a single scientific basis for the Ethics of the One and the Ethics of the Many. I am far from saying that Physiological Analysis may not be of the utmost service in defining, resolving, and generalizing by Concrete Analysis conceptions of conduct between Individual and Individual, which at present are utterly vague and even nameless. It is even possible that a kind of Physiological Ethics may yet falsify the opinion that 'there cannot be moral relations apart from society.'* But whatever be the character of this Physical Morality based on the evolution of the bodily organism, it seems to me destined to be as purely

---

* G. H. Lewes, *Problems of Life and Mind*, vol i. p. 173.

Relative, as certainly Unabsolute as the most ephemeral Ethics of the most ephemeral social relations. We may compare sensation and idea side by side, and restore the one by the aid of the other; but to track the one into the other and reach unity seems to me only an attempt to think the Absolute alone—an attempt which the whole history of mental evolution proves to be a failure—an attempt in fact to think the unthinkable, to think without Comparison and Contrast. Moreover, it would be difficult to imagine how a bundle of sensations, if we suppose the Ego to be nothing more, could historically and analytically resolve its own composition into material elements. It follows that if the dogmatism of the Intuitional School is objectionable, the dogmatism of the Materialistic School is infinitely more objectionable.

I do not say that Mr. Herbert Spencer seems to contemplate the reduction of *all* Ethical ideas to the evolution of material organism, but I think there is much in his *Data of Ethics* to suggest that inference. The phraseology and ideology employed are continually physical—the definition of conduct, 'an aggregate of interdependent actions performed by an organism,' the conception that 'greater organic evolution is accompanied by more evolved conduct,' the ideal chain of such evolution, from an infusorium up to the highest of mammals. But it seems to require little reflection on the meaning of the abstract term Life—a word which, in certain materialistic theories, seems to play the part of 'Happiness' in Ethics, or 'Wealth' in Political Economy— to see that the adjustment of the Individual and the Species to their Environment, will not create an Absolute System of Ethics or Universal Rules of conduct any more than discarded conceptions of Natural Justice and Natural Rights. The reconciliation of the interests and end of the Society or Species to the interests and end of the One do not seem to me more likely to be effected along the *apparently* rigid lines of Physical Evolution than through the palpable artificiality of the Utilitarian System.

This fundamental Ethical problem has, in fact, been attacked from all conceivable sides—the Individual, the Social, the Physical—with apparently little result, and with little result, just because these attempts have almost always been accompanied by a more or less conscious effort to transcend experience. While on the one hand Intuitional systems of Ethics have often cut the knot by simply declaring that man's true interests lie outside the sphere of his associations altogether, and then transferring into that sphere *à priori* conceptions of an Ethical Ideal beyond it, and, on the other hand, the harmony of human interests and ends can, of course, be only imaginary in any Ethical theory based on Social Life, so long as that life contains the most ample proofs of real discord, it seems utterly improbable that the Physical Evolution of Man and the Human Species will ever demonstrate the Harmony of Social and Individual Interests by an Absolute Unity of end for both.

I am not certain that I understand Mr. Spencer's meaning, but some passages in his essay seem to imply that there is an *Absolute* end for Social and Individual life, that this end is the same for both the One and the Many, and that

some higher evolution of conduct will reach that Ideal Harmony. For example, speaking of 'the several influences which have conspired to make men ignore the well-working of relations between feelings and functions,' he says* :—
'The ethical theories characterized by these perversions are products of, and are appropriate to, the forms of social life which the imperfectly-adapted constitutions of men produce. But with *the progress of adaptation, bringing faculties and requirements into harmony,* such incongruities of experience, and consequent distortions of theory, *must diminish;* until, along with *complete adjustment of humanity to the social state* will go recognition of the truths that actions are completely right only when, besides being conducive to future happiness, special and general, they are immediately pleasurable, and that painfulness, not only ultimate but proximate, is the concomitant of actions which are wrong.' This passage, and many others in the *Data of Ethics*, forcibly recall the proposition in the *Observations on Man*, that 'the rule of life, drawn from the practice and opinions of mankind, corrects and improves itself perpetually, till at last it determines entirely for virtue, and excludes all kinds and degrees of vice.'

It seems from passages such as these that the harmony Mr. Spencer has in view consists in the perfect Physical and Mental adjustment of each and all to the Social Environment; and the hypothetical part of this harmony is the assumption that the Mental and Physical, the Social and Individual Evolution of humanity tends towards that com-

---

* *Data of Ethics*, p. 99. The italics are my own.

plete adjustment. It seems to me that the Historical Evolution of man in society does not warrant this hypothesis. It has been the striking conflict of Social with Individual interests that has forced the Three Problems into prominence, and created the various systems of Egoistic and Altruistic Ethics. And now comes a final physical solution, a kind of physical gospel with these glad tidings—A golden age is coming, in which the desiderated harmony shall arise through the adjustment of functions to feelings and society to its environment. At first sight this hypothetical end and unity may seem to be only a kind of Relative Absoluteness, and to mean nothing more than an Ideal Harmony of society with its conditions; but there lies behind this harmony another principle which forbids us to regard the Social Ideal as merely Relative, and forces us to define our conception of Evolution itself.

The Ideal of a society with United and Harmonious interests is by no means new; it is as old as Ethical speculation itself. The novel feature is the assumption of a *Natural Physical* evolution towards the *human* attainment of that Ideal; and it is this very assumption which, on the one hand, appears to link the evolution of society with the Absolute, the Materialistic Absolute, by implying the existence of a Natural Force carrying on this evolution of conduct by such operations as the Survival of the Fittest, and, on the other hand, appears altogether to outstrip the legitimate range of Hypothesis. I do not believe that the conception of Evolution is synonymous with an assumption of Universal Knowledge; but I do believe that the conception of a Force Naturally producing Perfection, whether that Perfection be Material or Mental Perfection, and the assumption of acquaintance with the *nature* of that Perfection, whether it be Physical or Mental well-being, can only rest *either* on an assumption of Universal Knowledge or on a stretch of Hypothesis which no Scientific use of the Imagination can warrant. The conception of Evolution, therefore, which seems to me to underlie the *Data of Ethics*, is either based on a Knowledge of the Absolute, or, if admitted to be Relative, is not supported by sufficient experience to come within the Scientific Method of the Imagination: in either case it will pass the limits of the Historical Method.

The Physical Ideal of Social and Individual Harmony, therefore, seems to be almost as unhistorical, as imaginary as the beautiful Garden of Pleasure into which Sin introduced discord. As we cannot conceive a beginning or end of Evolution, Material or Mental, so we cannot conceive any Absolute Ethical System Physically founded on 'the complete adjustment of humanity to the social state.' The irregularity of Social and Mental evolution, upon which the Historical Method is based, does not seem to be destined to disappear with the absorption of the now lower grades of society into the now higher. There seems to be no reason, or very little reason, for supposing that if these lower grades should pass away, there will not continue to be like irregularities at higher social levels; or that, even if the whole Species were merged into One Society, no irregularity of Individual development, such as that which makes each living society now present types of the most various grades, would survive. If

Mr. Spencer means that there is a "gude time comin",' when the interest of Society and the interest of the Individual shall be Physically and Mentally one, and when the Evolution of that Social Harmony shall be reflected in minds that know, and bodies that act in accordance with it, I can only say that such an earth-paradise seems little less hypothetical than any heaven-paradise ever conceived, and in the rigid lines of its physical form decidedly less attractive. We, of course, believe with Mr. Spencer, that 'a rationalised version of Ethical principles will eventually be acted upon,' but the application of Physical Science to Ethics does not seem peculiarly fitted to effect this end. If Mr. Spencer would or could clearly distinguish the Social and Individual life from 'their environment,' a possibility which the condition of thought seems to negative, or prove that the forms of society are the result of physical laws, or that the adjustment of society to its environment is a law at all, or at least, that it possesses any *definite* meaning, we might be inclined to accept the philosophy of the *Data of Ethics*. Meanwhile we can only regard the Physical Ideal as a Materialistic analogue to the Ethical Systems which have been based on assumed acquaintance with the Mental Absolute—more historical but scarcely less hypothetical, almost as imaginative, though scarcely so dogmatic. And as regards the *practical value* of a conception which spans whole ages of future evolution, and seems to create a materialistic substitute for immortality itself, we shall believe that the Ethics of Free Labour and Free Trade, and the assumption that such Freedom will harmonize Social and Individual interests, is far more likely to influence men, and far more human than any irony of Materialism that seems to dress out the very ideals of human life in fine grave-clothes.

It is needless to say that I am not so ambitious as to suppose that I can draw an outline of the Ethics of the Future, based, as I firmly believe the science will be based, on the Historical Method. But perhaps something like the following may happen:—We shall start with an elimination of those Ethical conceptions which can be proved to belong to alien states of society. We shall formulate some principle which appears to be relatively the best for existing social conditions. We shall define our Ethical ideas and language by strict reference to that principle, but at the same time never lose sight of its Relative character. In a word, we shall admit the dependence of our moral standard on the good of the given community, and the relativity of that good to the organization of the community itself. If, for example, we admit that the good of society as at present constituted is the utmost Efficiency of Free Mental and Manual Labour, we shall form our Ethical theory and define all its parts by reference to that end. Should we regard such an end as ignoble, we shall take comfort from the Relativity of its origin and infer the possibility of its improvement. We shall recall the history of earlier moral theories, how humble their origin, how irritating to the sentiments they displaced, how dignified they since became.

> 'These that have it attained were in like case.'

We shall refuse to regard as a mean doctrine the belief

that our best ideals must be developed from our own Personal and Social life, and that our highest morality comes not from East or West but from within us, and around us. Will such a doctrine incapacitate us from cultivating self-control, from forming moral ideals for ourselves, or from appreciating the real value of the ancient? Can our Europe of to-day offer no ideal like the village commune of the Semites twenty-five centuries ago?

> 'Is all our light
> The glow of ancient sunsets and lost hours?'

If so, we shall admit that we have lived into insupportable conditions under which we have skill enough indeed to shatter the ideals we received, but not enough to create a substitute. But it is not so. Already, as we watch the rise of Ethical conceptions inferior to none the world has ever known—the growing honour, I had almost said divinity, of labour, the contempt for idleness, the growing respect for personal nobility, the contempt for merely inherited—we need not fear to own that we, too, morally and mentally, are the children of our social conditions, and that for us no less than for primitive man the saying of a wise poet is true,

> 'As what he sees is, so have his thoughts been.'

I say, therefore, that the Historical Method in Ethics is not only the best method of discovering the real Ethical theory of any given society past or present, but that it is the best method of discovering that Ideal which social conditions may admit, thus uniting the purposes of a science and an art ; and that, while its own progressiveness accompanies the Evolution of Society and Mind, it places all Ethical conceptions in their true light, and dishonours none because they happen to belong to social states that have passed away, and to have survived into conditions to which they are no longer applicable.

CHAPTER III.

THE HISTORICAL METHOD IN JURISPRUDENCE.

IF it be granted that the Historical Method is the true method in Ethics, no serious objection can be urged against its application to the kindred science of Jurisprudence. Indeed it is the progress of Jurisprudence which has done more to create the Historical Method than that of any other science, Philology excepted. The order of that progress has been from defining the rule of Legislation to analyzing Positive Law, and from the analysis of Positive Law to the Historical Evolution of Law. We shall now take a rapid glance at the work of the three great pioneers to whom that orderly progress is due.

Anyone acquainted with the tone of French Social Philosophy in the second half of the last century, the tone peculiarly marked in the writings of Jean Jacques Rousseau, will recognise the kind of speculation which, by force of repulsion, contributed to produce the doctrines of Mr. Bentham. The English theory of Representative Government, then, as now, far ahead of the reality, the theoretical rule of a Popular Majority, the absence of any defined principles of Legislation, and the presence of Legislative and Judicial confusion and abuse—these, with the French influence already noted, seem to have been the chief causes which produced the first practical theory, the first science and art of English Jurisprudence. But the Greatest Good of the Greatest Number is an end of Legislation and Social life, which itself needs a great deal of definition. In fact, there is scarcely a word in the famous formula which does not demand analysis, and which, when analyzed, does not reveal the looseness of the social theory it generalizes. What is Happiness? Why, it is relative to the society selected, to the individual selected, to the time, and to the place. To ignore that relativity is to ignore the most formidable question in Ethics—the question whether the interests of the One and the Many are identical. This is Mr. Bentham's grossest error—an error which underlies all his 'moral arithmetic,' and it is grossest just because it attempts to slur over the hardest problem of morals. Are your interests and mine identical? Are our interests those of the society to which we belong? Are the interests of our society the interests of the world? That is the problem which Mr. Bentham's units of pleasure and pain merely conceal. For, what is the tacit assumption upon which those units are based? The identity of Happiness for all men, that is, the identity of their Interest. If we are *assuming* that identity, if we believe that diffusion of knowledge will prove that identity, we ought to boldly state our assumption and belief, we ought not to leave them to be dragged out like a pair of lurking conspirators. The word, the conception Happiness, therefore, requires to be translated into more definite words, more definite conceptions. You may call it unanalyzable, you may invest it with the vague dignity of an Ultimate Truth, but you will gain nothing but obscurity by this unhistorical treatment. We shall examine further on the Economic translation which the idea has received.

But suppose our idea of Happiness to be clearly defined, suppose the Happiness of the One and the Many to be proved identical, whose definition, whose principle of identity, is to be accepted as the rule of conduct, of Legislation? Is it that of a philosophic clique, or is it that of the people? Can the Will of the Majority be in all cases the Greatest Good of the Greatest Number? Or must it be pared into precision and truth by a knot of *savants*? And if the people are the true masters of the government, what security is there that the knot of *savants* will persuade the masses to their own good? If the principle requires definition, so does its practice.

Although the idea of a thoroughly democratic machinery of government seems to have floated before the mind of Mr. Bentham, and contributed to suggest his doctrine, I do not remember in his writings any indication of his having regarded his Philosophy of Legislation as relative to social condition in its origin and application, as an unabsolute truth inapplicable to many ages and societies, and as in reality amounting to a theory of social life, its end and the means of effectuating that end. Mr. Bentham's theory is indeed open to many palpable objections besides those already noticed. For example, if the Greatest Number happened to be one social class, are the interests of society the interests of that class? Is the Greatest Good of society the good of that class? And is the Greatest Happiness principle compatible with

Class Legislation? Many like problems would have started up if Mr. Bentham's intolerable dogmatism had not precluded him from a dispassionate examination of the ideas he contemptuously rejected—a dogmatism which obscured the relation of his own theory to existing social conditions. If he had openly allowed that the Will of the Majority is the rule of Legislation his philosophy would not have been less dignified, and might have been much more fruitful. It would then have followed that the standard of Legislation must be the Public Opinion of the given society, and that the real and ideal qualities of that standard must vary with the quality of Public Opinion. The dependence of Legislation on social conditions would then have followed as a matter of course. The Historical Evolution of such social conditions would next have attracted Mr. Bentham's attention, and his theory, duly defined, might have assumed its proper place within a duly limited science of Social Evolution.

Yet Mr. Bentham's principle undefined, unhistorical as it was, had done excellent work. For the first time the practical Legal bearing of Ethical theory had been clearly proved. A step, a very decided step, had been taken towards a social science. And while the law reformers were exemplifying the force of the new principle, the generalizations of Positive Law were undergoing an analysis which was to display the necessity for historical treatment in a new light. To examine the actual analyses of Mr. Austin does not of course come within our scope. What concerns us is rather his non-recognition of the relativity of that analysis, his apparent belief in legal generalizations applicable to all states of society, and the absence of historical treatment which has produced these results. The great Jurist who is the third of our 'august triad,' Sir Henry Maine, has called attention to the first and third of these critical points. He has, for instance, shown that Mr. Austin's *determinate* human superior from whom all law is assumed to emanate is not historically to be found in all stages of society, and that 'the possession of physical power, which is one characteristic of sovereignty, has, as a matter of historical fact, repeatedly been in the hands of a number of persons *not* determinate'; that 'the capital fact in the mechanism of modern states is the energy of legislatures'; and that until the existence of the social state which this fact implies, 'the systems of Hobbes, Bentham, and Austin could not have been conceived.'

But I must regard the Universal aspect of Mr. Austin's 'General Principles' as offering a still more important *point d'appui* for adverse historical criticism. I do so because the admission or denial of this Universality, however cautiously expressed, involves radically different conceptions of the nature of the Historical Method itself. The fact is that neither Mr. Bentham nor Mr. Austin discarded the search for Absolute truth, for truth universally applicable. It is all very well to repudiate or even to ridicule, as the former ridicules, the conception of Law Natural; but what is the use of rejecting that ancient and respectable dogmatism in order, with Mr. Bentham, to transfer its pretensions to an insolent upstart, or, with Mr. Austin, to deck out the unabsolute results of Comparative inquiry in the borrowed nature of the banished abstraction? The belief that Comparative inquiry will give us principles universally applicable is as unhistorical and deserves as stern reprobation as the most audacious assumption of Intuitionists. The idea that we approach nearer and nearer to Absolute Truth by a wider and wider range of Scientific Comparison appears to me a deadly error in science, and almost as illogical as the denial of the existence of Absolute Truth. If the latter is mere dogmatism, so is the former. For to suppose that we are nearing Absolute and Universal Truth we must imagine that we see it, or, at least, know where it is. By comparing French, German, English, and Roman Law, we may of course obtain new lights, may generalize, may analyze our legal conceptions better. But only on one condition will those generalizations and that analysis be practically valuable, viz. that the Comparative Method has involved no radical differences of social life. The worth, therefore, of the new generalization, the new analysis, depends on their harmony with the structure of that society to which they are intended to be applied. The Comparative Method, therefore, and the principles it discovers depend alike for their materials and the value of their general reasoning on social conditions, and can never generate out of such materials generalizations *universally* true. The value of the Comparative Method is thus dependent on Social Evolution, and the principle of Montesquieu is never to be forgotten, 'les lois civiles et politiques de chaque nation doivent être tellement propres au peuple pour lequel elles sont faites, que c'est un très-grand hasard si celles d'une nation peuvent convenir à une autre.' This limitation of the Comparative Method I must regard of the utmost practical importance at a time when so many suggested reforms, legal and otherwise, are put forward almost solely on the recommendation of Foreign Parallels.

But just as Mr. Austin's Universal Juristic Principles were to be evolved by the Comparative Method, finding its requisite materials in French, English, German, and especially Roman Law, so his method of analyzing jural conceptions was to be Comparative. Is the abstract conception of Ownership to be analyzed? Then let us first examine the analyses which other systems have offered. No one will object to this method when properly limited. And as we have seen, there *are* limits to its application—historical limits. The idea of Ownership, for example, is not the same in Russian Village Communes, under English Land Law, and under a System of Tenant-Right. The analysis of legal conceptions in any age must partially depend on the Classification of society, just as we shall find that the Economic analysis of the abstraction Wealth is largely directed by the same Classification. The Clan age has its own Classification of society; the age of Slavery its own Classification; the age of Feudalism its own Classification. To mingle the unhistorical analyses of law belonging to different social states, and apply the result to the elucidation of our own legal abstractions *without historical discrimination*, would be as if, in order to analyze the Ethical conceptions of our own day, we were to throw aside all distinctions of social conditions, and jumble up Inherited Sin, Vicarious Punishment, Communal Responsibility, and minute discussions of Intention.

It is the Historical Jurisprudence of Sir Henry Maine which corrects, on the one hand, Mr. Bentham's unhistoric though systematic Ethics of Legislation, on the other hand Mr. Austin's unhistoric though Comparative analyses of Positive Law. Philology had in the meantime displayed the working of the Historical Method in some of its branches, and the recognised dependence of Language on the growth of society was certain to be followed by the recognition of the relation of that social growth to thought itself. At the same time the Greatest Happiness principle had been assuming more definite proportions; improvements in Legislation had been followed by improvements in the Machinery of Legislation, and the Reform Bill had put a new life into the principle. The Repeal of the Corn Laws showed the force of Public Opinion still more clearly, and Legislation then definitely translated the abstract formula of Benthamism into the more concrete shape of an Economic Maxim which tacitly underlies a mass of recent enactments—the Greatest Efficiency of Labour at the Least Cost. Although the philosophy of Sir Henry Maine has *chiefly* treated of Historical Jurisprudence, he has indirectly contributed much to Ethics and Political Economy. In fact it was *impossible* to admit the historical relativity of Juristic thought to the conditions it typifies without, consciously or unconsciously, extending that relativity to the whole range of Social Science. For example, a cluster of conceptions finds its nucleus in the social organization of Communal Villages. Partly Religious, partly Jural, partly Ethical, partly Economic, partly Psychological, the confused cluster of conceptions exemplifies the early confusion of unanalyzed thought as well as its relation to social life. Then the line of survivals, which connects as it were by stepping-stones the different stages of social evolution, conducts us at last into our own social life, and forces us to inquire whether the thought of our own time does not partially imply a similar origin. Nor has Sir Henry Maine refused to carry into the living processes of thought that method which he has wielded with such dexterity and success in analyzing the phenomena of Ancient Law, Early Institutions, and Village Communities. The modern history of the Law of Nature, the modern influence of Oriental on Western thought, and like subjects discussed in his works, are so many excursions into the present along the lines of our past history.

Yet, with the highest respect for Sir Henry Maine, I submit that the Historical Method is very far as yet from having developed its richest fruits, and the evolutionary aspect of his writings assures me that he would himself repudiate finality either for his method or for its results. It is with a like repudiation of finality, and a firm conviction that the general truth of my theory will be best confirmed by wider expansion and deeper analysis, that I offer the following criticisms on the state of the Historical Method as exemplified in the works of that eminent Jurist.

I. It seems to me that until the Historical Method is definitely united with the Philosophy of the Finite, of Experience, neither that Philosophy nor that Method can cease to be indefinite in their scope and vague in their results. In criticising Mr. Austin's use of the Comparative Method I have illustrated this indefiniteness, and shown that it leads to the re-establishment under other names of those imaginative and universal assumptions which have played so large a part in the development of all theories. The popular belief in an actual collision between theory and experience is only one of the widely ramifying results of too imaginative theorizing.

Without attempting at present to discuss the historical relation of a science to an art, I can only say that this supposed collision has reacted most confusingly on popular and scientific thought. When by the Comparative Method we reach General Legal Principles true of the conditions they represent, when by the same method we suggest Legal Reforms, and when by the same method we trace the Development of Legal Conceptions, are we to say that our method is changing because its end is changing? Are we to suppose that the Comparative Method is one thing while it traces the growth and decay of Physical and Mental Myths; another thing when it constructs a theory of modern Ethics; one thing when it constructs legal theories, legal ideas belonging to past conditions into some larger theory of Legal Development; another thing when it compares the legal theories of living nations with a view to progress or reform? I think not; I think that whether applied to the past, the present, or the future, the Comparative Method is one and the same, and that whether the intention of its use be practical guidance or theoretic accuracy it is still unchanged. As long as any doubt is entertained on this point it seems to me impossible to define the Comparative Method or its relation to the Historical — a relation which I conceive to be that of a species to its genus.

In the first chapter of his work on 'Village Communities' Sir Henry Maine briefly discusses the character of the Comparative Method in a manner, as it seems to me, indistinct and unsatisfactory. According to the opinion there expressed, the Comparative Jurisprudence, whose chief function is 'to facilitate Legislation and the practical improvement of Law,' is not the same as that which aims at describing the Historical successions of Jural conceptions; and it is said that this latter method 'is not distinguishable in some of its applications from the Historical Method.'* I submit that this view of the Comparative Method and its relation to the Historical is vague and misleading. It is no doubt a merely verbal question, whether we should call the Method which analyzes and theorizes the Evolution of Society and Mind (so far as it is dependent on social relations) by the name Comparative or Historical; and perhaps the name Comparative would be less liable to suggest the erroneous impression that the past alone is contemplated as its sphere. Yet so far as the verbal question is concerned, I am ready to defend my terminology. For, on the one hand, the most general characteristic of the entire method is Historical and Empirical, *inquiry by experience;* and, on the other, there is one phase of that inquiry to express which the word Comparative ought to be reserved. But this verbal point is not the point at issue. The real question is this—

* Pages 1–10.

Does the Comparative Method, as employed upon living institutions and modes of thought for purposes practical or speculative, differ at all essentially from the Comparative Method as applied to the Social and Mental phenomena of the past, for the purpose of putting those phenomena into their true order of succession? I believe that there is no real distinction, and that the evolution of Society and Mind prove that there is none. The idea that such a distinction exists appears to me to have originated in the conception (as old at least as the Roman lawyers) that the Comparative Method may arrive at Universal Principles, or Generalizations universally applicable. As far as unconsciously or unscientifically used in the past, the supposed universal generalizations of the method have been or are being historically disproved; but the idea still lives on, that the scientific use of the Method in the present—that use which contemplates the Political, or Ethical, or Juristic theory and practice of the future, may attain the universal dignity from which such conceptions as the Law of Nature have been historically deposed. As long as this idea is still retained, it will be impossible to regard the Comparative Method which explains the past and the Comparative Method which explains the present as other than radically distinct. But since it is clear that a belief in universally applicable generalizations evolved from particular social conditions is a contradiction in terms, I have no doubt that the imaginary double aspect of the Comparative Method is destined to vanish.

But a few examples will illustrate more distinctly the falsity of the supposed distinction. It is the uneven, irregular progress of society and mind that is the *raison d'être* of the Comparative Method no less than the Method of Survivals. If we compare two institutions or modes of thought for *practical* purposes, and if these institutions and modes of thought represent *exactly the same degree* of Social and Mental Evolution, no new light will be gained. It is the *contrast* of different Social and Mental conditions that strikes out the new light, and suggests the larger theory. Now let us compare two institutions or conceptions, in order to discover the *historical succession* they represent. Our purpose is indeed different; it is all science, all theory—no art, no practice. But the reason of our success, if any, is the same, viz., the contrast of different conditions, Social or Mental. For example, we wish to discover in a certain society the historical succession of ideas of ownership from the customs of a Village Commune to a system of Competition Rents. We have isolated proofs of different stages—rules of tillage evidently communal, references to restrictions on the alienation of land, fictions allowing the relaxation of those restrictions, allusions to customary payments for the loan of land. By comparing the social development of another country we wish to historically construct the exact lines of that social evolution with which we are dealing. It is plain that if we can only compare *exactly the same* social stages with only the same causes and the same results, if in fact the associations of the points compared are identical, our comparison will profit us nothing. I say, then, that in filling up the gaps in the Historical Evolution of a given society by aid of the Comparative Method, an element of *contrast* is essential.

Without this element no addition to the theory of the given social evolution can be reached.

At first sight it might seem as if the practical use of the Comparative Method as distinct from that commonly known as Historical were based on the reverse of this. For, unless the social states represented by two given institutions or modes of thought are *similar*, they cannot be theoretically compared with any practical result. For example, if you are constructing a theory of Ownership under Peasant Proprietary, you cannot derive much assistance from the corresponding English legal conception, except in so far as the elements of Scholastic Philosophy and Feudal Custom which it contains have been supplemented by the Commercial reforms of a new Social State. On the other hand, if your Comparative materials do not extend beyond two systems of Peasant Proprietary under exactly the same social conditions, and representing exactly the same stage of Social Evolution, you cannot hope to add anything to your theory of either. While, therefore, the *practical* value of the Comparative Method depends partly on *Similarity*, it also depends partly on *Contrast*. But the element of *Similarity* is also essential in recovering the *Historical Succession* of Social and Mental phenomena by that use of the Comparative Method which does *not* aim at any *practical* end. For, if in a given society we are attempting to reconstruct the stages through which the adult conception of Contract was reached, and if these missing stages are attempted to be filled in from the known development of the Conception in a country whose social evolution has been totally different, or at least essentially different, nothing but the most egregiously unhistorical confusion can result.

It follows that the Comparative Method, as applied to past and present, for theoretical or practical purposes, is one and the same, implying in each case elements of *Similarity* and *Contrast*, and in each case deriving its value from the same source, viz. the inequality of Social and Mental progress, one *part* of living society, though the whole is apparently moving in some uniform direction, being constantly behind or ahead of another part, and one *part* of defunct society, though the motion of the whole seems to have been likewise uniform, having been also behind or ahead of another. And although the *ends* pursued in the two uses of the Comparative Method seem to be different, the difference is more apparent than real. For when the practical end is reached the theory is verified by practice, and becomes historically true; and when the theory of past historical succession of phenomena is true, its basis of truth is the existence of corresponding practice : in either case, therefore, the end is to reach the practical, to reach experience, but in the one case the Comparative Method hypothesizes on future, in the other, on past experiences. If the theory of the past development of a country is true, then all the generalizations which are grouped together under that theory represent experiences real, practical. If the theory which declares the end of our living society to be the Greatest Efficiency of Mental and Manual Labour is correct, then the future experiences it foreshadows and assumes will practically prove its truth. The true theory of a living society, therefore, writes its history beforehand and outstrips experience; the true theory of a dead society writes its history behindhand and recovers experience; and the Comparative Method can both outstrip and recover the development of experience.

We must, therefore, regard Sir Henry Maine's actual distinction of two kinds of Comparative Method, and implied distinction of both from the Historical Method, as displaying no certain conception of the Comparative Method and its true relation to the Historical—no certain conception of the kind of truth these methods can discover, and of the reason for that discovery in their relation to Social and Mental Evolution. It must be admitted that these are serious objections against any Philosophy of Law, and I feel sure that Sir Henry Maine himself will be the first to admit their serious character. Until the scope of the Historical Method is clearly mapped out, until the kinds of truth it contemplates and the kinds of truth it does not contemplate are fully recognized, until the reason for its existence and the limits of its subordinate parts are understood, and until the explanation of Historical Method as an analysis of Social and Mental Evolution takes its place as the proper Introductory Chapter of Historical Jurisprudence, no sound Philosophy of Law seems possible. That unhistorical theorizing in Jurisprudence which Sir Henry Maine has done more than any living thinker to annihilate is sure to steal back through some side-door as long as the evolutionary relation of the Historical Method to Mind and the relativity of Historical Truth are not vividly realized. In fact the growth of Generalization is at this moment everywhere tending to construct 'Laws of Nature' differing only in name from that which Sir Henry Maine so felicitously reduced to historical phenomena. It is under the idea of a Social 'Law of Nature' that visions of future Ethical Perfection rise before the Evolutionary Moralist; it is under the idea of a Social 'Law of Nature' that the optimistic Economist prophesies the Harmony of Human Interests in the gospel of Free Labour and Free Trade: it is under the same idea that the Comparative Jurist sees in the widening range of his generalizations a kind of earthly ascent to that ever-receding heaven of human thought—Universal and Eternal Truth; and it is the Historical Method, and apparently the Historical Method only, that will control the impatient efforts of reason and imagination to pass the limits of Experience and to reach the Absolute by the plain proofs of their past futility.

II. The uses to which the Method of Survivals has been put by Sir Henry Maine, Sir John Lubbock, Mr. Tylor, Mr. Spencer, Von Maurer and a whole host of continental writers, is well known. It is a method at once remarkably philosophic and most unphilosophically indefinite; nor can I at present recall any decided effort to remove that stigma by any of the brilliant thinkers who have applied it to almost every range of social inquiry. Accordingly, both the name and the method are rapidly acquiring an indefiniteness which bids fair to rival that of 'Mythology'; and since the most magnificent myth is nothing more than a cluster of mental survivals supported on imagination, to cut short the growth of indefiniteness in the one case is to do it in the other also. To employ the method and phrase without attempting to limit their application and meaning is actually discreditable to Science. At present there is a lurking fear, not by any means groundless, that the meaning of the method is that any institution, any belief, may be relegated to the limbo of survivals by the magic touch of any *savant*. As long as this feeling exists, a degree of indifference will manifest itself towards results quite scientifically accurate, and the most absurd assertions will continue to throw discredit on the whole method. The method may be applied to the disentombed records of the oldest Semites, to the Philosophy of Greece, the Law of Rome, or the every-day thought of our own century; yet, no matter how interesting the results, so long as it is left undefined in scope, vague in origin, fluctuating and even palpably absurd in use, no higher logical place can be assigned it than that of a mental toy, beautiful, amusing, but scarcely more than a wonderful toy. It was with this belief that I attempted to find the origin of Survivals in the uneven evolution of society and mind. It is a plain fact that within our own society there are individuals who typify degrees of social and mental evolution from a comparatively low to a very high degree. It is a plain fact that around our own society and including it there are societies which range from almost the lowest to the highest yet evolved. In all these societies, in all the individuals of whom they are composed, there is a life of mind and action varying from the most complex to the most simple, and a progress of some kind varying from the most rapid to the almost stationary. It is this uneven progress that presents the scientist with Survivals, and assures him that phenomena so thickly scattered over past history, and so profusely discoverable in the present, cannot with any great rapidity vanish in the future. The *cause* of Survival, therefore, is the Relativity of individual and social progress.

But what will justify us in calling this or that institution, this or that belief, a Survival? Why does the Economist call the expressions 'Favourable' or 'Unfavourable' Exchanges by that name? Because his theory, his idea of Commerce, has developed; because the theory he repudiates as a Survival belongs to the childhood of Economic Science; because he now has a wider mental vision than they who still think as those expressions imply. But he does *not* mean to say that there are none who think any longer in the Survivals, the Myths he disowns; his repudiation is only relative; it only applies to those who have the same range of vision, of Economic *theory* as himself. There are not many who recognise *this* Survival either in thought or speech; but there *are* many who will at once allow that they do not any longer believe that the sun 'rises' and 'sets.' Why this difference? Because the relativity of thought has undergone a change; because the few who at first disbelieved the 'rising' and 'setting' of the sun have grown into a multitude; because the theory of the Few has become the theory of the Many.

Let the Survival be an institution. The Roman lawyers who watched the fall of the Republic might have anticipated that the system of *Responsa Prudentum* would cease if the rising Empire were finally established. If their theory was that the Empire *would* be established, then already the system was *for them* a Survival—a Survival on its way to death. Institutions and modes of thought around us are open to the same remark. The theory of the observer may regard them as Survivals; his theory of future progress may already have mentally displaced them. But will his individual theory, will the theory of a whole group of like individuals be sufficient to stamp on the given institution or belief the character sought to be affixed? In the mind of the thinker it will; in minds developed like his own it will; but to others his belief may appear even absurd. It is as possible to anticipate Survival as to be late in its recognition. To ignore this relativity of Survivals is also to miss their origin, to impress men with the idea that there is no deep meaning underlying the conception after all, and to delay the recognition of the fact that a Philosophy of History is at hand.

There is a theory of History which is based on the tacit assumption that Historical truth is some exact reproduction of facts in words. What is a fact? A thing *done*, you say, surely there can be no doubt about that. Well, and so these things *done*, these *dried facts*, are to be carried about in a linguistic dress, and the best *Historian* will keep such precious entities as distinct as possible from all inferences, from all theories of their relation, and by a skilful manipulation of his authorities sort out the driest fragments of past human experience. Is *this* History? Put the bones of a skeleton together, and you have *only* a skeleton. What a wretched painting of a human body that would be in which the artist had forgotten to fill in the flesh, and skin, and eyes! How horribly inhuman, how unhistoric, how false! But *Historic* truth is no more a mass of dry word-facts, no more a word-photography of events in the past than in the present. If so, the whole of past History would be a chaos of disconnected events—a chaos which could never be conceived in any but a chaotic conception.

But it is impossible for man to reproduce in thought a single fact without consciously or unconsciously associating it with others. Each mind that attempts to picture for itself the events of contemporary or past history, of personal or collective history, will be forced to compress the facts with which it is familiar into the framework of some portable theory or generalization consciously or unconsciously present. From abundant statistics, drawn with laborious care—statistics dependent on innumerable modern improvements in communication and science—we infer with doubt and difficulty a general theory of commerce, and correct its aberrations. We thus scientifically write our social history, expand our imperfect generalizations, and consciously correct them by fresh appeals to Experience. The generalizations which the social history of the past contains have been obtained likewise, only roughly, unsystematically, unscientifically, imaginatively. It is the task of the scientific historian to recover the missing links in the actual genesis of these rude generalizations; and while he does so by the aid of Comparison and Survival, while he does so by analogies from social evolution similar to that which he is analyzing, he recovers the theories of earlier thought with the same great instrument as that by which he must now construct a theory of living Ethics or Jurisprudence.

The Method of Survival, therefore, belongs alike to the past and to the *present;* it is relative to the Society and the Individual, to the Mind of the Society and to the Mind of the Individual. That Method, therefore, must play an important part in the formation of all sound theory of the present as well as the past. And while it is plain that there must be Survivals to one mind which are *not* so to another, to one society which are *not* so to another, to one part of a society which are *not* so to another, no danger will arise from this necessary result of social and mental evolution, provided its cause is constantly kept in view, and the relativity of social and individual progress never forgotten.

I have taken some trouble to explain my theory of the cause and effect of Survivals, not because I think that Sir Henry Maine has misunderstood their nature or misapplied their Method, but because by leaving that nature and that method unexamined he has, with a large number of recent writers on Social Evolution, exposed his theories to adverse criticism. By far the greatest example of a Survival which the works of Sir Henry Maine present is the Conception of a 'Law Natural,' which he has traced to its historical origin with a degree of elegance and discrimination scarcely to be paralleled. Now, what is the full meaning of a belief that this 'Law Natural' is a Survival? You will find the authority of that 'Law' fully recognised in very recent Continental and English authorities on International Law, on Municipal Law, on Jurisprudence generally, and not by any means forgotten in every-day appeals of legal pleading. There can be only one inference. The Survival *is* a Survival only for a certain development of Juristic mind. It is far from being such throughout Jurisprudence; it is farther from being such in the practice of the Courts; it is farthest from being such in the thought of the masses.

I conceive, therefore, that Sir Henry Maine's use of the Method of Survivals is incomplete, because it does not point out their relative character, the cause of their existence, and the consequent dependence of this branch of the Historical Method on the Evolution of Mind.

I have now stated several objections, as I conceive them, to Sir Henry Maine's use of the Comparative Method and Method of Survivals. The Methods of Concrete Analysis and of Scientific Imagination might, indeed, be easily illustrated from his works; but they have not been used as *methods*, and it is unnecessary to recapitulate similar objections. It is true that the greatest problems of the Historical Method have not been solved by Sir Henry Maine—its relation to Mind, to the Association Philosophy, the limits of its use, the subordination of its parts. It is true that he has not attempted to answer several questions which his own admirable works suggest—for example: Does Sir Henry Maine believe that the origin of *all* conceptions can be traced to Social relations, to certain forms of Society; or does he intend to imply that only one class of Mental Phenomena is due to such relations? Does he intend to anchor Social Science upon Physical or Physiological Laws—Laws of the material forces of Nature or Laws of the material functions of Man? Does he intend to separate his science from associations which do not owe their origin to any Social Classification? In a word, does he intend to cut off from Historical Jurisprudence all that mass of Mental Phenomena which is centred in the life of the Individual, and which is and has been the constant subject of Juristic speculation? Or does he intend these to come within Historical Jurisprudence as a chapter on Mental Physiology?

But however unhesitating I have been in the expression of this criticism, I cannot but tender my respectful and heartfelt thanks to the great Historical Jurist who first taught me, in company with many another, wherein consists the true meaning of Historical Science. And if a Philosophy of History is ever founded in this country, I cannot help believing that its origin will be due to the Author of the '*Ancient Law*' in a higher degree than to any professed historian.

CHAPTER IV.

THE HISTORICAL METHOD IN POLITICAL ECONOMY.

THE science of Political Economy, aiming as it does at analyzing an abstraction, Wealth, has pursued in various directions all the three possible methods of that analysis. There have been some who have regarded the science as Deductive, in the sense of starting from general principles of mind, and among these some have declared that these principles were inherent in Human Nature, others have not been anxious to go further than to assert that they are part of human nature without discussing whether that nature itself depends on social conditions. For such Economists some leading principle of human action in Commerce, such as that men buy in the cheapest and sell in the dearest markets, that, in other words, they *always* act from Self-interest, is proclaimed *the* generalization from which each separate truth in Economic Science may be inferred, or at least into which every separate truth may be resolved.

Others, without at all abandoning this last opinion, find the pivot of Economic Science to be the Natural properties of Land, its limited extent, its limited fertility, and constantly there moves before their eyes the struggle of Population to overleap the limits of Nature, while prudence persuades them against the attempt, or death, like the king-of-the-castle in the game, throws them back. This is the Physical aspect of Economic Science. These are the limits which the Physical Nature of Man and the Physical Nature of the World set to the multiplication of men, that is, to the growth of social numbers.

On the other hand, besides the Mental Nature of man, besides the Physical Nature of Man, and besides the Physical Nature of the World, there is another pivot of Economic analysis which has exerted as powerful an influence. The relation of Wealth to the Structure, the Classification of the society whose laws of Wealth were to be discovered, influenced from the first the development of those theories which are generally known as Economic. I do not say that this relation of social organism to Economic theory was by any means *consciously* recognized. Just as the conscious contrast of lower social types has displayed the relativity of Ethical thought, just as the conscious contrast of lower social types has displayed the relativity of Jural conceptions, so it was not until many differences of social organization had been forcibly realized as producing different Economic relations that the Comparative Method revealed this relativity of Economic thought. This is the point at which an intention has been displayed by a well-known School to merge the science of Political Economy into that of Social Evolution. For my own part, it seems to be clear that Political Economy must have a separate existence so long as it can be shown that the phenomena of Wealth are distinct from other sets of Social phenomena; and, since no reasonable doubts can be entertained on this head, Economic Science may be best regarded as one of the chapters of Social Evolution, but none the less a *distinct* chapter, with *distinct* facts and *distinct* theories of its own.

From the third stand-point of the science the statistics of social life assume immense importance, and the science becomes Deductive in a totally different sense from that in which the term is applied by the *à priori* Economists. Deduction now becomes the reversal of Induction, and the process of descending for verification to fresh statistics from a generalization which has itself been evolved from the same source makes the science 'Deductive.'

Thus there are Methods of Economic reasoning which may be regarded as purely Deductive in the sense of purely *à priori*, thus making the science a Mental science; purely Inductive (as supplemented of course by the reversal of the process), and, therefore, making the science a science of social relations without seeking any absolute causation for these relations either in Mind or Matter; purely Materialistic, thus regarding the framework of society as thrown into its existing shape at a given time by Physical causes of Human or External Nature; and there are composite theories combining all or any of these methods, Physical or Mental, in different ways. It is clear, therefore, that should any law or theory of Political Economy under such conditions be called 'Natural,' it will require some examination of the theory to decide whether the 'Nature' in which it is believed to be rooted is the 'Nature' of an Eternal Mind, of an Uneternal Mind due to inherited associations, of the Social Man—that is the Social Body generally—of the Individual Man, of the Physical organism of Man, or, finally, of the Physical combinations of the external World.

The result of these varying and contradictory methods is the present state of Economic Orthodoxy, if indeed any such Orthodoxy can be said to exist; and I shall now attempt to show this and *en passant* to illustrate the Economic bearing of the Historical Method by a miniature picture of Economic Orthodoxy so far as its outlines are not utterly obscure.

Since Wealth is an abstraction, and the Science of Political Economy is nothing more than a theory of the Production, Distribution, and Exchange of Wealth, it might have been imagined that the mere definition of the science would have been sufficient to establish its relative and unabsolute character. For it is plain that the concrete phenomena which are summed up in the abstraction Wealth are far from being the same in different stages of society, and that the abstraction not only changes with time, but as applied to different social groups, or widened into a conception of all existing social groups, will include contradictory phenomena. What is Wealth to the Coral-islander may not be Wealth to the English merchant; what is Wealth to the German of to-day might not have been Wealth to the German of Tacitus. If this relativity of the conception had been recognized, the historical evolution of the social and mental phenomena which Political Economy undertakes to explain could not have been overlooked.

As it is, the science, as an Orthodox Science, possesses a very varied aspect. The analysis of the Production, Distribution, and Exchange of Wealth has been performed from three different stand-points, the Physical, the Mental, the Social, each characteristic of three different schools of thought, just as it has been observed that the same triple stand-point of philosophy is more or less visible in Ethics and Jurisprudence.

I. The first problem which arises in Political Economy (assuming Wealth to be defined, which it has never been— a definition of which, indeed, could only be the work of the Historical Method, and would be strictly *relative*) is the Production of Wealth. What is the cause of that Production? Very little reflection, it would seem, is required to observe that the causation depends partially on the Individual Mind, partially on Social Combination, that is, the Organization of Society, and partially on Matter, the Physical properties of the Physical materials employed. If all these causes could be reduced to One Principle—if, for example, the peculiarities of Individual Mind could be reduced to Social Organization, and Social Organization reduced to the influence of Physical Forces, or if Social and Individual Mind could be reduced to Physiological Laws, and those Physiological Laws reduced to the Laws of Physical Nature— then the triple stand-point of the science would have been avoided, just as the same unity of causation would affect all other branches of Social Science.

But it is by no means to be supposed that this tripartite

character of Economic Science and its methods has been recognised within the circle of Economic Orthodoxy. Far from it. The question, What is the cause of Production, has scarcely been *definitely* asked. Accordingly, the answer which, in their own way, the Physiocrats gave to that question, the answer which the Father of the science gave, and an answer which is a kind of convenient receptacle for all other answers that may be given, have left their impress on the theories of the Orthodox Science, and the methods of the Orthodox Science.

The principles of the Orthodox Science may be briefly expressed in a single sentence : there are 'Natural' Rents fixed by 'Natural' fertility, a 'Natural' rate of Profit, a 'Natural' rate of Wages, and, as a consequence of these three 'Natural' abstractions, a 'Natural' Incidence of Taxation. I think that this sentence contains the whole theory of Orthodox Economy, and that this theory depends on the confused use of three different Economic methods, and three confused answers which have been given to the question, What is the *cause* of Production ?

The answer of the Physiocrats was brief—Land. The common sense of Adam Smith rejected that answer; his own was also brief—Labour. Another answer brings up the rear—Capital. Before I connect these answers with the triple character of Economic Orthodoxy, I wish to ask, What would be the most logical mode of solving the question ? It is plain that the Production of Wealth depends upon the Efficiency of Labour, but the Efficiency of Labour is only another abstraction. Analyze it, and there turn out to be three factors in the Efficiency of Labour; 1st, the Mental, Individual and Social; 2nd, the Physical properties of Man, Individual and Social; 3rd, the properties of Physical Nature. Without attempting to show the relations of this analysis to historical evolution, I shall now return to the answers of Economic Orthodoxy, and attempt to prove the confusion of results which their unanalyzed combination has produced.

It is true that no exponent of the Science affirms any longer that *all* Production of Wealth depends on Land, but the relation of Land to Production is none the less the recognized pivot of Economic Orthodoxy. First came Malthus, whose Theory of Population limited the growth of the Human Species by the 'Natural' fertility of the soil. If it had been more observed that this elastic limit of Efficient Labour is really dependent on the Mental and Physical qualities of Man and Society, as well as the 'Natural Fertility,' and that this 'Natural Fertility' is constantly becoming less 'Natural' under their effects, the gloominess of the Malthusian Doctrine might have been greatly lessened. But no; the properties of 'Nature' and the phraseology of the Physiocrats diverted attention.

Next came the Theory of Rent, which, though older than Ricardo, is yet too strongly associated with his to be ever connected with another name. The 'Natural' fertility of the soil now assumed a more social aspect. No longer only the harsh mother of over-population, famine, and crime, Nature smiled on the owners of the broad acres as their peculiar protectress—at once the source and the defender of their social existence. If Malthus had presided over the infancy of Economic Orthodoxy, an unsavoury infancy, Ricardo was now to preside over its youth. Under his care the relation of Production to Nature became the central conception of the Science. Malthus had only connected Society generally with the principle, had only shown that the numerical expansion of Society was under its control. But now the theory was applied to explain the internal classification of society, which, in other words, meant the explanation of the social Distribution of Wealth. In criticising Mr. Herbert Spencer's Ethics, I have adverted to an apparent law of thought which forces us to analyze generalizations by social classifications or physical facts. As a part of the Historical Method of reversing the actual evolution of mind, I have called this apparent law the Method of Concrete Analysis. Now, as long as the classification of society remains vague, any abstractions which depend on that classification must be also vague. It will be evident, then, that if any limits, fixed by Physical or Human Nature, can be discovered for any *one* class, an important step will have been made towards clearing up the whole group of social abstractions which depend on social organization. This fact of mental evolution enables us to understand at once the relation of Ricardo to his predecessors and to Economic Science. If the amount of rent, 'Natural' rent depends on degrees of Natural fertility, if the degree of Natural fertility at a given moment in cultivation depends on the Demand of Population, and if the price of agricultural produce depends on the marginal land which pays no rent, the 'Natural,' in the sense of Physical, evolution of the Landlord is proved, and a 'Natural' limit at once drawn round *one* class of society.

It is not at present my purpose to criticise this theory of Ricardo, but, admitting for the moment its truth, it is evident that the already recognized tendencies of Profits and of Wages to equality need only be supposed actual facts, and rigid lines of demarcation between the classes of society will have been established. In this way the Natural rate of Profit, the Natural rate of Wages, and the Naturally limited Rent give definiteness to the otherwise vague abstractions included in the more general abstraction Wealth, and assume sharp lines of distinction between the social classes whose concrete existence underlies the abstract analysis. It seems strange that Ricardo did not himself by the mere reasoning of his results become the founder of Historical Political Economy, and recognise the relativity of his own social analyses to the concrete classification of English society in his own day. Had he looked across the Channel to examples of Metayer-Tenancy, or Peasant-Proprietary, or Village Communes, no doubt could have been left that his science was unabsolute, its truth relative, and its method Historical. But the immobility of his own 'Natural Fertility' seems to have settled on his mind, and the 'Natural' limit to the Efficiency of Labour seems to have acted as a barrier beyond which he would not or could not see.

However, the idea of the paramount importance of Land as an agent in Production had now done its greatest work: it had given a show of Deductive accuracy to the science, and linked its leading theories to a supposed unchanging principle—a kind of principle which, whether material or spiritual, attracts thought with magnetic power. When it is remembered how much of Economic Orthodoxy is built upon the Theory of Population and the Theory of Rent, I think it will be allowed that the tacit wish to construct a Deductive science from an absolute principle of Matter underlies the whole of Orthodox Economy. We shall now see that the second answer to the question, What is the cause of Production, ramifies no less widely through the science.

The conception that Labour is the cause of Wealth, brought so prominently forward by the Father of Political Economy, lost ground by the rise of the Ricardo-Malthusian School, and was indeed never conceived at the earlier epoch in its true social aspect. On the other hand, it assumed at its first re-appearance the doubtful attitude of a social heresy loudly declaring that, since all Wealth was due to Labour, none but Labourers had any right to share in it. It was thus in connexion with this communistic application of Economic Theory that the Distribution of Wealth and the cause of that Distribution, the second great doctrine of Economic Science, passed from scientists to the people. The conflict of this popular principle with the Theory of Rent displays one of the most remarkable interactions of scientific and popular thought that any age has witnessed.

The Theory of Rent, by the inferences which it admitted, had however done much to clear the way for its rival. It had indeed been a corollary of the Rent Theory that rent does not enter into the cost of agricultural produce, the cost being fixed by that part which is raised at the highest cost, and this part, by the theory, paying no rent. But at the same time it could not be disguised that since the difference between the best and worst lands in cultivation fixed rents, and since the increase of population tended to augment this difference, and since the Law of Population declared this increase to be against the interests of the people, the same physical properties which allowed the Landlord his rent without hurting anyone also made his interests hostile to those of the community. For was it not his interest to prevent the Free Importation of corn, and force the people to limit their numbers and the efficiency of their labour by the extent of these islands? And was it not *their* interests and the interests of efficient labour to throw open the ports, and to increase with cheaper food both their numbers and the efficiency of their labour? If the Landlord had been given a *carte blanche* by Nature, they, too, could retort with 'Natural' rights, the 'Natural' rights of Labour. And since society was founded on Labour — it is a short distance in some minds from social wealth to society itself—the enemies of the interests of Labour were the enemies of the interests of Society. A few faint efforts were made to show that this inference from the Ricardian Rent Theory was false, yet the theory itself true, but the contradiction was too glaring.

Everyone knows what has been the effect of this uprising of Labour. It has done marvellously. Since the Repeal of the Corn Laws a new Ethical spirit has been breathed into English Legislation; it is the spirit of Bentham, but it is his spirit in an Economic dress—the dress of the Economy of the People, the Economy of Labour. The degradation of that term now reaps its vengeance, and the Economy of *Labour* is not so much regarded as the Economy of Mental and Manual Labour of all sorts, as the Economy of the harder sort of Manual Labourers, who, at the same time, are the largest class. Whatever be the apparently glorious future of Free Trade—and I would be the last to say a word against a principle which seems destined to expand into a veritable Philosophy—we cannot close our eyes to the fact, that if the Economy of Labour is to mean the Economy of any one class, we may prepare ourselves for the rise of a new class despotism, worse than the former, because it will be more absolute, and for the destruction of Free Trade itself the moment that class believes its interests to be jeopardized.

In the face of such possibilities, the answer that Labour is the source of Wealth ought to be carefully reviewed. If the influence of the conception has shown how well it fits into popular associations, it has also shown that the associations it may be made to fit may be too narrow. In order to reduce this narrowness to its truly erroneous light, we must simply ask again, 'What is the Cause of Production?' At once it will be seen that not even *all* labour, Mental and Manual, of all descriptions, can put forward with truth the claims advanced by Manual labour alone. It is not a fact that Land is the source of all Wealth, but it is almost as far from being the fact that Labour is the source of all Wealth. Here, for example, steps in the third claimant to the causation—Capital. Who is he? What is he? An abstraction—Wealth laid aside to assist future Production, so that until we are sure of our Proteus Wealth we have no chance of catching his partner. We have therefore returned to the point from which we started, the abstraction Wealth and its fluctuating concrete phenomena. If Capital be a cause of the Production of Wealth, it is clear that the effect is in this case its own cause. Are Land and Labour likewise Wealth, and likewise their own causes? Let us try whether the second problem of Orthodox Economy may be able to settle this question for us, and in doing so illustrate the relation of the science to the Historical Method.

II. This second great problem is: What is the cause of the Distribution of Wealth? It is in the answer this problem has received (if anywhere) that the need of the Historical Method ought to have been felt, and, as a fact, has been felt. Economic Orthodoxy has, as we have seen, analyzed the Production of Wealth by the existing phenomena of its Distribution. By doing so, in spite of loud-sounding claims to Deduction, it had tacitly adopted the Historical Method, and analyzed the abstract by concrete phenomena, and through concrete classification. But now, when the second problem arises, what was to be done? The classification of society had been already utilized, it had served as the analysis of Production. What was to become of Distribution and *its* cause? What, in fact, was the cause of the existing Economic classification?

Here was an opportunity for bringing the Historical Method to the front. The Freedom of Competition between class and class and the elimination of Custom had to be recognized as the fundamental principle of distinction. Without this Free Competition, Orthodox Rents, Orthodox

Wages, Orthodox Profits could not exist, all the elegance of Economic Theory would vanish, and nothing but the confusion of lawless wages, profits running wild, rents going up and down as they pleased, could remain. The disorder was too horrible to contemplate. The assumption that Competition *is* perfectly free, and Custom *is* perfectly absent, was made, the ideal and imaginary nature of the hypothesis excluded from view, the evolution of Competition out of Custom unhistorically neglected, and Competition itself formulated as a law of Mind and the Law of Political Economy—the Law of Buying in the cheapest and Selling in the dearest market. This Law is simply the theory of Self-interest, only unlike its Ethical analogue, Benthamism, it does not directly say anything about the relation of Individual to Social interests, its stand-point is in fact that of the *Individual* trader, while that of Mr. Bentham is the stand-point of Society. It is extremely interesting to watch the manner in which these principles have been silently blended. It is true that few writers or thinkers boldly face the assertion that the interests, the Economic interests of the One and the Many are the *same*, and that there is no collision between the Economic interests of different men and different societies. A famous French Economist has indeed made the establishment of this Harmony of Interest the thesis of his works; but the brilliancy of his treatment has not concealed its defects, and the leading maxim of Economic Orthodoxy still wears to some degree the unbenevolent aspect of Egoism.

But it is not the Ethical aspect of Free Competition

that at present concerns us; it is rather the relation of the assumption to existing society, to past society, and to the probable future. The Orthodox Theory is that, eliminating certain causes which produce differences in wages, all wages tend to be equal, and so, for scientific purposes, *are* equal; that all profits, allowing for mere temporary fluctuations, tend to be equal, and likewise *are* equal; and that the Free Competition of Population with Capital, in the one case, and Capital with Capital in the other secures the general level. A German School of Economists, whose best known representative in this country was the late Mr. Cliffe Leslie, assailed and carried with ease these weak defences, and did so by a slight application of that Method for which I am now contending. Comparing the actual rates of wages in the same country, at given places and times, it was easily shown that the assumption of Free Competition possesses the most mythical, the most imaginary qualities. The same line of argument could be readily turned against the theoretic equality of profits. Finally, the path which Sir Henry Maine's masterly analysis of 'Natural Law' had disclosed lay ready for the Economist to take, and it was at least as easy to prove that Free Competition had been historically evolved out of past Custom as that its assumed universality is false. In fact 'Natural' wages and 'Natural' profits collapsed before the Historical Method in Political Economy as completely as the Law of Nature had collapsed before the same method in Jurisprudence. The extent of the ruins, however, seems scarcely yet to be realized by the assailants or their opponents, and I shall therefore turn aside for a moment to examine them.

As long as the 'Natural' rates of Wages and Profits were believed in, the classification of society was rigidly marked out by Economic Science. The status of farmer as receiver of his 'Natural' agricultural profits was clear; so of the manufacturer as the recipient of *his* 'Natural' profits; so of the agricultural labourer and of the artisan as recipients of *their* 'Natural' wages. And since Physical Nature herself had set bounds to the Landlord as an abstract personality, the definiteness of the economic abstractions—Rent, Profit, Wages—had followed from the limits which Nature and Competition had set to their concrete causes in Social Classification. It was in this way that the abstraction called the Wages-Fund had been reached, and it is here that I am able to fulfil my promise to connect the principle that Capital is one cause of the production of Wealth with the Historical Method, and to show why it is that Capital being defined as Wealth is also regarded as a cause of its own production.

The abstract conception of the Wages-Fund has been reached by a mental process strongly reminding me of Mr. Mill's conception of Happiness. In the latter case, Happiness represents the sum of Pleasures looked at in the Concrete, and the conception is regarded as indeed an abstraction but a concrete abstraction—an abstraction representing concrete phenomena viewed collectively. Just as this conception gathers up the various kinds of Pleasure into one, so the theory of the Wages-Fund gathers into one heap, as it were, all the wages given throughout a country or countries or the World—the weakness of the generalization growing with the extent of its application—and boldly affirms that the Law of Distribution is not in the actual distribution as affected by local and temporary causes, but is to be found by dividing the wage-receiving population into the sum of the Wages-Fund, and calling the result *average wages*. Thus in a manner remarkably resembling the Utilitarian Moral abstraction, the Economic abstraction was reached by mentally connecting into one concrete mass all individual wages and all groups of wages. There are two assumptions underlying this Economic theory, both of which are cut away by the Historical Method, and each of which, being the counterpart of the other, shows the necessity of analyzing an abstraction by the reversal of its historical genesis.

The first assumption is that Competition has been *equally* operative over the whole field from which the various heaps of wages are gathered into the central concrete abstraction. This assumption is necessary in order to maintain the second assumption which is its counterpart, viz., that the mere division of the sum called the Wages-Fund by the wage-receiving population gives the actual Law of Wages. I say therefore that the genesis of the abstraction shows the necessity men are under of analyzing by reversing the historical development of their abstractions, and I say that the Economic generalization of Economic phenomena into Wealth, the Ethical generalization of Ethical phenomena into Happiness, and the Juristic abstraction of the Greatest Good of the Greatest number, all exemplify, like the Wages-Fund, the action of this mental evolution. I think I can also show that this necessity for the historical reversal of the generalizing process, in order to explain the generalization itself, follows from the nature of generalization, and therefore of reasoning. For what is the *petitio principii* inherent in all reasoning? The ultimate universal abstractions evolved from particular phenomena. The only explanation, therefore, which can be offered for such abstractions must lie not *beyond* but *below* the abstraction. The process therefore of reaching the abstraction is the reverse of the process of explaining it, and the process of explaining it is the reverse of the process of reaching it. As part of the Historical Method, I have called this process the Method of Concrete Analysis, and I think that the position of Capital as its own cause and effect is cleared up by this method.

Capital, being that part of Wealth which is laid aside to assist future Production, the abstraction is part of the largest abstraction of Economic science, viz., Wealth. If it had been reflected that not until the result of this laying by has been *experienced* can the question of Productive or Unproductive employment be settled, the Empirical and Historical character of Political Economy would have been more apparent. Why is it then that Capital is its own cause and effect? On the same principle that Wealth must be its own cause and effect. The abstraction Capital, like the abstraction Wealth, simply sums up all known causation in their respective Economic spheres, and therefore when we reverse the process, and seek to explain the abstraction, we can only repeat the empiric causation which it includes. The Historical Method, therefore, as I conceive it, seems to reveal the whole genesis of Economic thought as well as the principle of progression underlying the changes of Economic theory.

This principle of change has been, as already observed, harder at work in the orthodox sphere of Economic Distribution than in that of Production. I do not know any better way of disclosing the ravages which the Historical Method has here made than by exhibiting the effects it has produced on the Orthodox Theory of Taxation. That theory is built upon the assumptions of rigidly marked Social Classification and perfectly Free Competition, both of which assumptions have been overthrown by the Historical Method. The Orthodox maxim of Taxation is brief and without much appearance of *Finanzwissenschaft*, as homely, in fact, as that which expresses the principle of Competition as Sale in the dearest and Purchase in the cheapest market: the maxim is simply that he who can throw the weight of taxation off his own shoulders will infallibly do so, and he who cannot will grin and bear. It had been early discovered that the *nominal* and the *real* payer of a tax are not identical. So the problem of taxation is to find the vents through which this shifting process goes on; to legislatively guard them; and then to tax away with the serene consciousness that the incidence of the tax is as clear as if it were being physically reviewed. In other words, the problem of taxation is this: given any tax, to find the *true* limits of its incidence. It is in fixing these limits that the limits set by 'Natural' Rent, 'Natural' Profits, 'Natural' Wages, have been to Economic Orthodoxy invaluable. I shall now attempt to prove this proposition at some length, for, as I conceive, no better evidence of the inherent weakness of unhistoric thinking in Political Economy can be produced.

From the first beginnings of Economic thought, theories of the incidence of taxation have been constantly wrecked. The Physiocrats, as is well known, believed that all taxation ultimately falls on Land. And if Land is admitted to be the sole source of Wealth, then taxation, being so much taken from Wealth, must necessarily be so much taken from Land. If, in the same way, it be granted that Labour is the sole source of Wealth, similar reasoning can be readily employed to prove that all taxation must ultimately fall on Labour. In all such cases the fallacy can be at once detected by the erroneous assumption that this or that source of wealth is the *sole* source. But although a theory that *all* taxation must by nature fall on any given class is not likely now to find much credit with anyone, there are fragments of such theories which can impose on the most acute minds by the elegance of their theoretic shape and the apparent worth of their practical applications.

For example, let a tax be imposed upon Rent, and the unhistorical theorist has his solution cut and dry for you at once. And this is his solution. The farmer must obtain *his* '*Natural*' profit—and is assumed to have been, before the imposition of the tax, in receipt only of that *Natural* profit, Why? Of course because the easy-going '*flow*' of capital into his abnormally profitable business would have soon reduced his abnormal profits. If he pays the tax, therefore, his normal profit sinks below the *Natural* level, and, of course—a rather jaunty assumption of free agency—he will prefer *and be able* to employ his capital where such profit can be secured. The farmer, therefore, must needs beg to be excused. Will, then, the farm-labourer pay the tax in diminished wages? Why, *he* must get *his Natural* rate of wages, and he, too, must be assumed to be in receipt of nothing more than this *Natural* rate (whatever it is). Why? Because, if his wages sink below that rate, an even more magical facility than the 'flow' of capital must waft him from his native village, and afford him that blessed haven of Natural Rate which he has had the intelligence, nay omniscience, to discern. The labourer, therefore, must also beg to be excused. And now the issue has been narrowed to a single alternative: the tax can only fall on the remaining classes—the landlord and the consumer—the latter abstract personality being synonymous with 'general community,' only affecting much greater precision and really disclosing the artificial character of the whole reasoning. Upon which of these two will the tax on Rent fall? Which unfortunate must draw the 'old maid' card? Now behold, says our Economic juggler, the consumer can, of course, only pay the tax in an increased price, of agricultural produce; but if the tax increase the price, it must fall on the margin of cultivation which fixes the price; but if it fall on the margin of cultivation, it must fall on the 'Natural' profits of those who pay no rent. Fall on 'Natural' profits! Goodness Gracious, who could entertain the thought! Presto Pass, Hocus Pocus! Gentlemen, the landlord has it. Q. E. D. And Economic Orthodoxy has done with *this* particular tax.

Now, in sober earnest—and it is a matter of very sober earnestness, seeing that the Financial System of our nation is directed and must be directed by Economic Theory of some kind, which must make itself felt most soberly in the pockets of those who shall feel the force of the maxim that the *Nominal* incidence should be assimilated to the *Natural*—in sober earnest, then, what are the inferences to be drawn from this very pretty theory, its neat compartments withal for Landlord, Capitalist, and Wage-receiver, and its ready transformation of all three into a fourth receptacle for all stray ills of taxation called the limbo of Consumers? (1) If all taxation has this neat *Natural* Incidence, the three classes, being supposed, prior to the imposition of any tax, to receive only their 'Natural' Rent and Profits and Wages, cannot be taxed *at all*, and taxation must entirely fall on our Protean friend the Consumer. (2) But this abstract personage is the whole community rolled into one; so we must draw Cobden's conclusion that 'every tax is ultimately felt more or less by everybody.' But this is to surrender the whole problem—to allow that our '*Natural*' Profits, Wages, Rents, have not carried us one inch towards solving the problem of incidence. Shades of Ricardo and Malthus! we shall be excommunicated from the dead and living fellowship of Economists if we adopt such an inference. (3) But we have scarcely wriggled away from—not out of—this difficulty before we are entangled in another. Taxation cannot reach *Natural* profits and *Natural* wages, yet it *can* greatly affect the consumer and his power to consume. But profits and wages greatly depend on the power to purchase commodities, the power to consume commodities—the Market, in fact; and if that power is lessened by taxation, the taxation must have a most unpleasant *Natural* incidence on both profits and wages. Miserere! Let us turn away. What next? (4) The fact is, there can be no need to employ any Canon of Taxation at all or to take the slightest trouble about the *real* incidence of a tax. Why? Because the tax must fall into the exact lines, pleasant or unpleasant, which Nature (that is, the Economist speaking with an almost theological inflatus in her name) has marked out. It matters not a straw, therefore, whether taxation be direct or indirect, controlled by central authority or left to local caprice, imposed on commodities or deducted from income. Briefly, *Laissez-faire* is the key to Finance.

What is the historical purport of this *reductio ad absurdum* of Economic Orthodoxy? That the rigidly marked lines of social classification, which are first *assumed* to be rigidly marked, and then applied to the analyses of the abstractions, Wages, Profits, Rent, as species of the genus Wealth, are not so 'Natural' as was supposed; that an *assumed* classification of society is the basis of Economic Orthodoxy; and that even if on that *assumption* the science were perfect, the progress of social evolution must itself introduce error. The science, therefore, must be admittedly based on a given social order, and the analysis of Wealth will change with the classification of that order, since it is by such classification that both Production and Distribution, the ascending and descending sides of the abstraction Wealth, so to speak, are analyzed into their smaller abstractions.

III. It has been shown how the Economic Orthodoxy of Production and Distribution proves the relation of the science to Social and Mental Evolution, and the necessity for Historical treatment. We shall now find that the same relation and the same necessity are observable in the third great Economic problem, and, as before, most observable in relation to taxation. This problem is: What is the cause of the Exchange of Wealth? It is only another way of asking, What are the causes which produce this or that ratio of Exchange? And since Exchange ratio is called Value, the problem of the cause of Exchange is the problem of Value. What is the relation of this problem to the two former, the problem of Production and the problem of Distribution? We shall not attempt to answer that question until a brief review of the Orthodox theory of Exchange has put us in a better position to do so.

The three Orthodox laws of Exchange—briefly, Demand, Demand *plus* Cost, and Cost—exemplify all the attitudes of Economic thought.

The theory of Value due to Demand or Monopoly is based on the absolute or temporary limitation of quantity fixed by physical causes—a limitation, in fact, which *man* cannot alter. This value is indeed primarily dependent on physical causation, but even the extreme case of absolute monopoly has also a side reference to the two other factors in Economic theory, the labour of man and the calculation or feeling of mind. For it is plain that, no matter how absolute the monopoly, the wealth which is offered for it, and therefore the labour which that wealth represents, must be decided by the means and the wish of the purchaser. We shall find that each of the Orthodox laws of Value possesses this threefold aspect, and it is the undue assumption of unity and neglect of this triplicity which underlies nearly all the Economic confusion on the famous topic of *Value*.

It is not, however, the extreme case of absolute monopoly in which Value is entirely dependent on Demand and Supply, that suggests the great discussions on Value; it is the second and third laws, the laws of Demand *plus* Cost, and of Cost alone. The law of Value as caused partially by Demand and partially by Cost ramifies throughout the whole range of Economic Values, and at the same time exemplifies its own relativity to social conditions. The most famous examples of its operation are, the Theory of Rent and the Theory of International Exchange; and since the artificial nature of the Rent Theory has been already illustrated, we shall select the Theory of International Exchange. The problem, What is the cause of International Values, cannot be reckoned among the settled questions in Economic Orthodoxy, but neither can the answers which that problem has received be excluded from any brief outline of the Orthodox Science. These answers notably exemplify the various stand-points of Economic thinking. For Adam Smith value in Exchange being based on Labour, the theory of International Exchange assumed the shape of a theory of Free Labour—its free division, its free co-operation. But if the question had been fairly asked, In what does the efficiency of Labour consist, Adam Smith would at once have seen that there are other factors in that efficiency besides the labour of man. Ricardo, then, taking up the theory where Smith left it, and turning to account the differences in Natural advantages which he had already used with such effect in his Rent Theory, based his International Value upon two distinct factors, the efficiency of human labour, and the differences of each country's natural advantages. The Theory, which Ricardo *illustrated* by a number of examples which like some illustrations of John Stuart Mill assume the air of *demonstrations*, is capable of being expressed in a single sentence; Each country will purchase in International Trade through those commodities in which its natural advantages make its labour most efficient, and will gain most by purchasing through such commodities others which it might have produced at home at less cost than they can be produced abroad, but to produce which its labour would require to be diverted from the production of those articles in which nature has made its labour most efficient. The Ricardian doctrine of Comparative Cost is, therefore, based on the combination of Natural Advantages and Human Labour, and is singularly in keeping with the Ricardian Theory of Rent. But just as Smith had regarded the problem of International values from the aspect of Cost as dependent on Human Labour, just as Ricardo had taken in the element of Physical Advantages, so there was a third stage in store for the theory depending on the third standpoint of Economic theory—Mind, the Wishes of Man. It was John Stuart Mill who brought this third aspect of International Values into prominence, and assigning to the law of Demand and Supply the priority, put more into the background the previously marked relations of International Values to Cost of Production. But the popular discussions of the Corn Laws had now forced into prominence a question which Ricardo had not even raised; the question was, What is the ratio of advantage obtained by each of the trading countries, and upon what causes does that ratio depend? And thus the novel features of John Stuart Mill's theory of International Values are its relations to Demand and Supply, and its attempt to solve this problem of Relative Gains. It is remarkable that the proposition which Mr. Mill borrowed from Mr. Senior, viz. that each country gets its imports at less cost in proportion to the general efficiency of its labour, did not show that distinguished economist the uncertain attitude of his International Exchange theory, and the effect of this uncertainty on the problem of International Finance. At once rejecting the notion that the real gains of International Trade consist of the merchant's profits, Mr. Mill found them to consist in the saving of national labour, and proceeded by this principle to trace the division of International gains. If Mr. Mill had devoted more attention to the three factors of International Value conjointly, he would have been forced to confront a fundamental Economic problem which he hardly ventured to approach, viz. the relation of natural monopolies to the efficiency of labour, and the attempt to solve this problem would have shown the insufficiency of the data upon which the Equation of International Demand and Supply is based. It is easy to show that Mr. Mill's theory of International Exchange involves a contradiction, and I shall attempt to show the existence of this contradiction by the attitude of Mr. Mill's theory towards International Finance. Inferring that the joint saving of labour effected by the exchanges of two nations, supposing trade to be confined to two, would be distributed between them in proportion to the efficiency of their respective national labour, Mr. Mill at the same time admitted that the nation whose demand for foreign goods is weak, while the foreign demand for its own goods is strong, gains most by the exchanges, and gains most in proportion to the relative weakness of its demand. Mr. Mill made no attempt to show that the *Efficiency of National Labour* and *National Demand* are one and the same; that attempt was reserved for Mr. Cairnes. Now, if the relation of International Demand is the law of International Values, it is plain that such a country as England, for example, by taxing a commodity like coal, in which it has a great natural advantage, and which is in great foreign demand, can throw part of its taxation on the foreign purchasers of its coal, without at the same time diminishing its own trade proportionately, so long as the tax leaves some margin of the International labour-saving to the foreigner. This inference is actually drawn by Mr. Mill in his *Essay on Some Unsettled Questions of Political Economy*. Passing by the disastrous effect of such a doctrine on the theory of Free Trade—it is not the only point in which Mr. Mill's Free Trade theory is heretical— it can be shown that this contemplated possibility of taxing the foreigner contradicts Mr. Mill's opinion that the gains of International trade fall naturally into such shares as the efficiency of Home Labour may determine. In order to do so we have only to call to our aid the theory of Profit. The 'Natural' rate of National Profit will depend on the efficiency of National Labour. Now if, in the case above put, England's tax on coals really did fall on the foreigner, those branches of foreign productions in which the tax was felt would have their profits decreased, and by the well-known Orthodox principle, which Mr. Mill would have been the last to deny, capital would leave these trades until their rate of profit had again reached the Normal National Rate. It therefore follows that the tax could not fall upon the foreigner except by decreasing his Normal National Rate of Profit, through lessening the efficiency of his national labour. But if so, the tax must lessen the means of the foreigner to purchase, not only the coals, as in our example, but all other foreign commodities; and, therefore, the country which has imposed the tax will merely lessen, in the long run, the demand for its own goods.

Without pursuing any further the many problems which Mr. Mill's theory of International Exchange would suggest, we may lay down that the theory, as it left his hands, held no definite place as regards Cost of Production or Supply and Demand. The problem now passed to Mr. Cairnes, and, with that remarkable sagacity which has placed him at the head of English Economists, he at once recognized the cause of Mr. Mill's confusion in his uncertain analysis of Demand and Supply, in his uncertain attitude towards the mental part of the science, and in his uncertain attitude towards the relation of national monopolies to International Trade. There is much in Mr. Cairnes's theory of Political Economy with which no Historical Economist can agree: for example, his attitude towards the Wages-Fund Theory, his opinion that Political Economy is 'neutral in the presence of competing systems of social life,' and his Economic attitude towards Deduction; but on the subject of International Trade he is infinitely the clearest thinker, not only among English, but any Economists with whose writings I am familiar. We have not space in so small a work to discuss his only half-developed theory of International Trade; but his proof that Demand and Supply are the same phenomena—his proof that the International theory of Comparative Cost is reducible to the triple law of Home Values, and his proof that the saving of labour cannot be the sole measure of International gains, have smoothed the way for a complete Economic Harmony of Home and Foreign Trade, and left the inference very plain that International Values and Home Values must be regarded, if they are to be understood, from all the three possible attitudes of Economic Theory.

Thus the Economic theory of Exchange Values has been growing fuller and fuller; but never was its relation to the Historical Method and the Evolution of Society and Mind more apparent than at this moment; and as it is on the field of Home Finance that the artificial character of Economic Orthodoxy is easily exposed, so it is on that of International Finance that the true nature of the problem of International Exchange is most manifest. This is best seen by examining such a Commercial Treaty as that of 1860. A slight inspection will show that it presents three features— a Protective, a Reciprocitarian, and a Free Trading; the treatment of French contrasted with Spanish wines, the bargaining about French silks and English woollens, and the balancing of French and English Excise, being examples of these features. But whatever survivals from exploded theories may appear in such treaties, it is manifest the relations of International Finance will create a whole mass of new Economic Thought as certainly as the relations of International Law have created a body of moral maxims. I shall not attempt to find the probable effects of the interlacing of National Systems of Taxation, which seems to be a destined concomitant of Free Trade, nor to forecast from such probabilities a future Economy of Free Labour; but it is clear that differences of National Indebtedness, of Local and Central self-government and the systems of taxation accompanying them, of natural advantages, including distances from the best markets, will prevent that absolute freedom of Exchange and Competition which is the ideal of one great body of International Publicists. It is enough for us to foresee a nascent mass of Economic truths, which will reflect the International Conditions of Society towards which Europe appears to be tending, and to infer in the future, as we have seen in the past, a body of Economic theory reflecting Social Conditions.

What, then, is the relation of the Orthodox Economic theory of Exchange Value to the Orthodox Economic theories of Production and Distribution, and in what relation do they all stand to the Historical Method?

The three laws of Value have the same threefold aspect as Production and Distribution, viz. Physical, Social, Mental.

Assuming a Freedom of Competition, which the condition of Capital, of Land, and of Population do not confirm, there has been mapped out a classification of society in regular lines; the concrete divisions thus marked off have been employed to analyze the sub-abstractions of the genus Wealth, and this analysis has then been applied to all social conditions. Thus, the absence of Custom and the presence of Unrestricted Competition having been assumed in Home Values, the same ideas are transferred to International Values, and the whole Orthodox Theory of International Trade is an *anticipation* of International *Free* Trade. While the *imaginary* and *hypothetical* character of these assumptions have been studiously kept in the background, the Comparative Method alike on the fields of Home and International Trade has been showing the artificial nature of the whole science, and in wider or more minute experiences has forced by *conscious contrasts* the recognition of Economic Hypotheses. Thus the application of the Historical Method to Economic Orthodoxy is being brought about by the evolution of society and the wider range of experiences that evolution offers. The unhistorical assumptions of the Ricardian School squandered, as we have seen, the most splendid opportunities for the creation of Historical Political Economy, and while they were constantly employing Hypothesis in a more or less Scientific use of Imagination, while their social analysis of Wealth was that of Concrete Classification, while the Economic principles they repudiated were the most remarkable examples of Survivals, and while Malthus and Smith had abundantly employed the Comparative Method, they failed to understand the methods they were employing, and exaggerated the worth of the truths they discovered. What have been the results of this *bouleversement*?

The Science of Political Economy has fallen almost into as great discredit as that of Ethics, and, by sheer force of repulsion, a school of Practical Economists who will not any longer stand by the Ricardian abstractions has arisen. The foundation of the Science in experience has had to be re-laid. And why? Because Economists have allowed their Imagination to altogether detach itself from Experience, and the ultimate inferences of their doctrines have actually contradicted Experience. From commonplace things of Earth— its customary wages and rents, its retail profits that defy calculation, and many other unknown or unknowable things, they suddenly clambered by a kind of bean-stalk contrivance into a goodly country, where all this sublunary confusion was transformed into the neat regularity of 'Natural' Wages, 'Natural' Profits, 'Natural' Rents, and 'Natural' Incidence of Taxation. But your fine discoverers had scarcely got up there till they began to quarrel about the exact ladder by which they had mounted, and while they wrangled about the merits of Induction and Deduction, their enchanted land wholly vanished, and they themselves came plump down into the world of common sense and experience. Such, if I mistake not, has been the progress of Economic Orthodoxy, and that progress, with its many 'Natural' prodigies, has been even a more fruitful warning against the unhistorical in Social Science than the Law Natural of Jurisprudence, or the many other 'Natural' wonders of Ethics.

CHAPTER V.

THE LOGIC OF THE HISTORICAL METHOD.

GROTE, in his review of Mill's Examination of Sir William Hamilton's Philosophy, recognizes the valuable service which Mr. John Stuart Mill performed in showing the relation of the Syllogism to Induction, and thus establishing the Unity of Logic. But it seems to me that this reconciliation, so deservedly applauded by Grote, goes far deeper than even the historian of Greece imagined. In order to show this, if possible, I shall briefly examine the relations of Induction and Deduction to that Historical Method which it has been the aim of the past chapters to partially illustrate.

I begin with Deduction. I do so because in the evolution of thought it was the earliest to exert a powerful influence. But I must define what I at present understand by the term. In one sense, that term is used to mean *à priori* reasoning, the explanation of phenomena by an assumption such as instinct or intuition, or a fragment of a Divine and Eternal Mind. In another sense, it is only the process of Induction reversed. For just as we form by Induction a generalization out of a number of particulars, so, when this end has been attained, we can descend again to fresh particulars; and while testing the truth of our generalization, allow by the necessity for that fresh test the presence of the *ultra-experience* or *imaginary* element which that generalization to be such at all must contain. It will not be supposed that the Deductive Method in the latter sense could have possessed any *early* importance. For, in this latter sense, that method implies the *consciousness* that particular phenomena *are* the source of the generalization, and therefore implies the recognition of Induction, the very absence of which recognition is the most striking characteristic of early thought. It follows that the Deduction which I have in view is synonymous with *à priori* reasoning; with this difference, that as a legitimate mode of reasoning, confined within the range of probabilities, it is now *consciously* analyzed; whereas the obliviscence or unconsciousness of the whole process was the essential characteristic of its use in the days of an almost uncontrolled imagination. To have *consciously* watched or historically reviewed the genesis of a single generalization would have sufficed to destroy an enormous mass of archaic thought. For example, the whole system of Platonism would have been impossible, had the source of the smaller abstractions out of which that system springs been distinctly visible. Similarly, it would have been impossible, in the face of such *conscious comparison and contrast*, for the idea to have been maintained that all knowledge must set out from generalizations. But this is the very idea upon which the Aristotelian Logic is built up. It follows that the analysis of generalization must throw a flood of new light on the nature of that Logic.

What, then, is the Historical Method but an analysis of Generalization, more or less complete? What, but our social prism for the decomposition of thought, splitting up the ray by comparison and analysis into imagination and reason, and marking the points of their blending and divergence by survival? As long, therefore, as Deductive or *à priori* reasoning was unanalyzed the Historical Method was an impossibility.

Now what is the *Historical* import of that Revolution in Philosophy which vulgarly finds in Bacon a kind of eponymous father? Surely it is nothing less than the recovery of the *Historical* genesis of Generalization? To maintain that new truths are discovered by Induction is simply to analyze the growth of Generalization from particular experiences; to allow the *Petitio Principii*, inherent in all reasoning, is to admit that the Absolute lies beyond our reach, to admit the Philosophy of the Relative, to admit the presence of an Imaginative element *in all reasoning;* and to admit that all Induction, all the Inductive Methods, are based on the idea of *Causation* is to approach very close to the rationale of the Historical Method. It is the analysis of Generalization which forms *the* basis of the Historical Method; the Scientific Method of the Imagination discloses and controls the necessary element of Hypothesis which binds in an implication of *causal* relations the smallest and the grandest of Generalizations; the Method of Survivals exposes the growth and decay alike of Experience and the Imagination it supports, explains the existence of Superannuated Reason, and forbids us to be shocked by the Relativity of truth our Generalizations contain; the method of Concrete Analysis is tacitly based on the famous Inductive formula that all reasoning is from particulars to particulars, and admits the principle that every Generalization to be decomposed must be resolved into these its original materials; lastly, the Comparative Method is nothing more than the Scientific use of Association, the Scientific recognition of Difference and Agreement, the outer and the inner relations respectively of every circle of Generalization. I say, therefore, that the Inductive Method and the Historical Method are to all intents and purposes one and the same, only with this difference, that the Method of Induction has never been recognized as simply the Analysis of Mental Evolution, whereas the Historical Method cannot be used much longer without that recognition. And since the element of *conscious* mental action is vastly superior to that of *unconscious*, the Historical Method, even if it did *not* suggest any new reasoning of its own, must be so much an advance upon the Inductive.

Roughly speaking, therefore, there lie within man's memory three ages of Generalization, marked respectively, as I conceive, by Deductive, Inductive, and Historical reasoning. The difference between the first and the second is that of a supposed and real ascent. Induction has pointed out the dangers of ascent, has devised sundry precautions and appliances to secure its safe performance, but the main difference after all is, that we start confessedly from the plain to climb the hill, instead of supposing as of old that the ascent had been already made, and inventing contrivances (very good in their way) for returning in safety with wonderful visions of other lands. A very reasonable result followed. Hill after hill was scaled inductively, but not an explorer returned with any verification of those ancient wonders which it was loudly proclaimed he *must* see, if only he mounted high enough. From the lowest sandhill to the loftiest summit within man's present reach Induction has led the way, but neither loftiest summit nor lowest sandhill has offered a glimpse of the promised sublimities or lost itself in another world. So the scaling parties have grown incredulous. They have refused to believe in the visions of their forefathers. They have done more. They have commenced to look about and ask how those visions came into being at all. On the plains and in the valleys of human Experiences they have picked up here a little, there a little, of that gorgeous scenery which they who had never climbed at all imagined into upper worlds of everlasting light. Was it to be supposed, was it to be wished, that all these magnificent creations of early imagination would instantly die off? No. The revolution in thinking which the rise of the Inductive Method marks was far from suddenly sweeping away all but its own creatures. But the revolution was none the less real because its progress was slow, and it was none the less a *recovery of unconscious mental evolution*, although a long time was to elapse before it was recognized as such. I repeat, therefore, that John Stewart Mill's reconciliation of the Aristotelian and Inductive Logic goes far deeper than the historian of Greece imagined, and beyond the reduction of both to the Philosophy of the Finite, clears the way for the recognition of both as analyses of Mental Evolution preparatory to the Historical Method.

Is the Inductive Logic, then, 'an inquiry into our idea of Cause' as Dr. Bain says: are we to admit with Mr. John Stewart Mill that the basis of the Inductive Methods is the law of Causation ? If so, the analysis of Causation is the pivot both for the Historical Method and Scientific Induction. What but the Law of Discrimination or Relativity is the reason of the Comparative Method? And while 'our knowledge of a fact is Discrimination of it from differing facts and the Agreement of it with agreeing facts,' if 'the only other element in knowledge is the retentive power of the mind or memory,' is not the recovery of that retentiveness the great work of Historical Analysis and the Method of Survivals ? 'When,' as Dr. Bain says, 'the logician speaks of a Notion, Concept, or Abstract Idea, he must not be understood as implying anything beyond the *agreement* of a certain number of things in a given manner.' Certainly. But can the logician or anyone else avoid thinking in their own several ways what *makes* the agreement be an agreement—what *makes* the difference be a difference ? And is not this the problem of Abstraction ? And is not the Abstract Entity to which Generalization seems to point a conception of *Cause* unconscious, vague, or scientific ? And does not the Logic of Induction abound with obscure recognitions of this ideal, this imaginative element—in Hypothesis scientifically controlled, in Analogy scientifically limited, in Approximate Generalization, in Probable Evidences, in the grounds of

Belief and Disbelief, in Fallacy, in Definition, in Classification—nay, in the inherent *Petitio Principii* of all Reasoning? And is it not the Scientific Method of the Imagination that reveals the unity of all these, and links in a vast Chain of Evolution the imagination of the modern scientist and that of primitive man?

The unity of Induction and Deduction is, therefore, but a stepping-stone to their union with the Historical Method and the gradual realization of the dreams of Guizot and Buckle—The Philosophy of History.

NOTE.

THE struggle between the Economy based on Human Labour and the Economy based on Physical Nature is the great debate of Continental Economists. A good illustration of the present state of the struggle is to be found in the chapter 'La rendita della terra' of Signor Garelli's 'Principii di Economia Politica' (Torino, Ermanno Loescher, 1875). The following quotation illustrates the author's standpoint :—

'Primieramente dobbiamo richiamare le considerazioni, che sin da principio abbiamo esposto intorno alle supposte *ricchezze naturali e gratuite*, che omai tempo è che cessino di ingombrare il campo della scienza. La natura non offre all'uomo che *utilità in potenza*, le quali non diventano per lui *utilità reali*, ossia ricchezze, se non a misura, che applica il suo lavoro alla loro *attuazione*, ed in ragione dell'entità di questo lavoro medesimo, il quale accumulato costituisce il capitale, e si accumula appunto dall'uomo il più possibile, perchè ne riconosce un aiuto indispensabile e potentissimo al lavoro ulteriore. La terra non è più una ricchezza gratuita, che un'altra qualunque, e in quanto si volesse considerare gratuita è a disposizione di tutti gli uomini tanto adesso quanto potè esserlo pei primi suoi abitatori, anzi possiam dire meglio adesso che allora, in ragione dei maggiori mezzi, che hanno di impossessarsene.' [Page 288.]

www.ingramcontent.com/pod-product-compliance
Lightning Source LLC
Chambersburg PA
CBHW030403170426
43202CB00010B/1467